FRESH IDEAS IN
LETTERHEAD &
BUSINESS CARD DESIGN 2

FRESH IDEAS IN
LETTERHEAD &
BUSINESS CARD
DESIGN 2

GAIL FINKE AND LYNN HALLER

ROCKPORT
PUBLISHERS

Dedication

To Meghan Nicole

Acknowledgments

Thanks to the talented designers whose work is reproduced here, as well as to the hundreds of fine designers who sent in their work for consideration. Thanks also to the judges who chose the winners, the designer who showcased them here, and the development editor who saw this project through to publication.

Fresh Ideas in Letterhead & Business Card Design 2. Copyright © 1995 by North Light Books.
Distributed outside North America by:

> Rockport Publishers, Inc.
> 146 Granite Street
> Rockport Massachusetts 01966
> Telephone: (508) 546-9590
> Fax: (508) 546-7141

This hardcover edition of *Fresh Ideas in Letterhead & Business Card Design 2* features a "self-jacket" that eliminates the need for a separate dust jacket. It provides sturdy protection for your book while it saves paper, trees and energy.

99   98   97   96   95   5   4   3   2   1

Library of Congress Cataloging in Publication Data

 Fresh ideas in letterhead & business card design 2/[written by] Gail Finke ; and [edited by] Lynn Haller.
>   p. cm.
>   Includes index.
>   ISBN 1-56496-156-7
>   1. Letterheads—Design. 2. Business cards—Design. I. Haller, Lynn
II. Title. III. Title: Fresh ideas in letterhead & business card design 2.
NC1002.L47F56 1995
741.6—dc20

>   94-37916
>   CIP

Written by Gail Deibler Finke
Edited by Lynn Haller
Interior and cover design by Brian Roeth

The permissions on page 136 constitute an extension of this copyright page.

Contents

The Elements of Letterhead Design   2

Successful letterhead design appeals to both your clients and your clients' clients. Mastering the elements of letterhead design and targeting them to your two audiences ensures success.

Low Budget   10

Great design doesn't have to be expensive to produce. Often tight budgets inspire creative solutions.

Type   52

More than simply a method of transcribing useful information, type can be a powerful element of any design.

Visual Effect   78

A bright color, an intriguing paper, or a unique illustration can demand notice in even the busiest office. Without words, visuals can instantly create a mood or communicate your client's personality.

Special Production Techniques   112

Foil stamps, die cuts, metallic inks . . . even one of these printer's techniques can form the nucleus of inventive designs that command attention.

Introduction

It's easy to underestimate the importance of letterhead design. Though a letterhead package doesn't have the glamour of a poster or packaging for a hip new product, it can mean the difference between success and failure for your client's business. A business card, a sheet of stationery, even an envelope can make that invaluable first impression that leads to further business — or the lack of it. Without a professional letterhead package, a small business might never attract the bigger, better-paying customers it needs to grow. And with the wrong look, no matter how attractive or functional, a business won't connect with its potential clients.

Computerization has made letterhead design simpler and more affordable. Ironically, it's given a boost to designers at the same time it's taken away some of their clients. Small businesses are now tempted to design their own stationery rather than spend money to hire a designer. The results, however, are usually amateurish. Businesses that do hire designers thus make an even better impression when clients compare their cards or letterhead with the competition's.

The projects in this book demonstrate just how much difference a well-designed letterhead package can make. From the letterheads alone, the businesses who commissioned them appear professional, intriguing, competent and interesting. Use this book to inspire you and to generate ideas.

Measure your own work against some of the best letterhead design today. And remember that your clients won't be competing against metalsmith Victoria Sadowski, photographer John Wong, Deleo Clay Tile, and the other businesses whose outstanding letterheads appear in these pages. Their letterheads will probably be judged against more ordinary competitors. So even one unique design element, special printing technique, unusual paper stock, or clever use of color will set many businesses apart from their competition and lead to growth, increased revenues and perhaps — for you — repeat business.

THE ELEMENTS OF LETTERHEAD DESIGN

Letterhead design is deceptively simple — and inestimably vital.

Compared with a major ad campaign or a thirty-page annual report, a letterhead system might seem easy. A sheet of paper, a business card, an envelope: what's to worry about?

Plenty. Each part of a letterhead system makes an indelible impression, often a first impression, on your client's clients. A poor, illegible, or wrongly targeted message can literally mean the end of your client's business. Rarely does a graphic designer have such power in his or her hands.

To use that power well, you have to follow a few simple rules. First, know your client. Second, know your client's clients. And third, make sure the name, address and phone numbers are easy to find and read. There's a lot more to good letterhead design, of course. But everything else hinges on these principles.

The Bones of a Letterhead System

Three basic parts make up most letterhead systems: the letterhead itself, the envelope, and the business card. Some businesses need only a card, and some only letterhead. It's hard to imagine a business that would need only an envelope, but one probably exists.

Some businesses, on the other hand, need more pieces for their letterhead systems. Notecards, second sheets for letters, labels, and postcards are all common additions. Depending on your client's business, many additional printed pieces may be necessary. And because letterhead helps establish and maintain your client's identity, it's usually appropriate to extend the letterhead design to any print graphics.

In the United States, the usual size for business letterhead is 8½" x 11" and the standard envelope is the old no. 10 (4⅛" x 9½"). Throughout the world, the standard business card size is 3½" x 2". These sizes adapt to innumerable design styles and printing methods, as the examples in this book demonstrate. But because the use of these same few sizes is so ubiquitous, a change in even one piece can help your client's stationery stand out from others. A larger or smaller letterhead, a different stock or custom envelope, a square or curved business card—any of these can make your client's business memorable.

The business card is an especially popular opportunity for creative treatment. The business card is usually the only piece of the letterhead system that anyone keeps, and most people have file boxes, wallets and even drawers full of them. Designers have discovered ingenious ways to make the business card memorable, from adding simple folds to creating tiny books, boxes, and other fold-out items. But beware the urge to experiment too much. Often, a business card that's too difficult to store ends up in the trash.

Know Your Client

Every business is unique; even the most mundane manufacturer or service provider is different in some way from its competitor. It's your job to find out what that difference is, and to communicate it in your letterhead design.

This kind of detective work helps ensure a good design.

Most owners are only too willing to talk about their business —why it was started, why it's different or better than others. If they don't volunteer this information, be sure to ask.

Besides knowing your client's business expertise and personality, it's also a good idea to find out about how they will use the end product you're designing. Do they use laser printers, ink jet printers, dot matrix printers, typewriters (yes, some small businesses

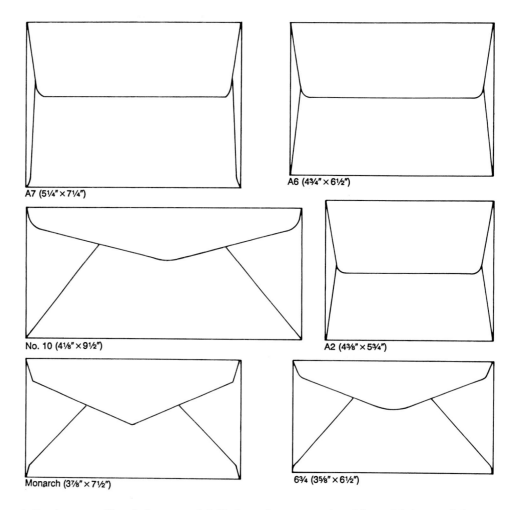

A7 (5¼" × 7¼")

A6 (4¾" × 6½")

No. 10 (4⅛" × 9½")

A2 (4⅜" × 5¾")

Monarch (3⅞" × 7½")

6¾ (3⅝" × 6½")

▲ Envelopes are either stock or converted. Stock envelopes are made and then printed; converted ones are printed then cut and folded. Stock envelopes are less expensive in small quantities and available with little lead time; however, they don't come in all paper grades.

You can have converted envelopes made from any paper, but it generally takes about four weeks. You'll also need to order about 25,000 to make envelope conversion a cost-effective option. The main reason for choosing an envelope conversion, however, is the printing technique to be used. Embossing, thermography and bleeds often do not work as well on stock envelopes.

still use them), or good old pens to write their letters? How often do they plan to use their letterhead? Will the company president or the secretary —or both—be using it? Will the business cards be handed out in person, or will people pick them from displays at shows or other gatherings?

To help assemble the information you need, you might want to make a checklist. If possible, go to your client's offices to see the decor—even if it's a factory or warehouse. This will tell you a lot about the personality and style of the business, and may give you a design hook. Look at your client's products or services. Study your client's existing letterhead design (if there is one), as well as that of your client's competitors (your client can probably furnish you with this). Then ask the following questions:

• What's your primary business? What makes it different from other businesses like it?

• How do you think you're perceived by your clients and potential clients? How would you like to be perceived?

• What do you like about your current letterhead? What do you like about other letterheads you've seen?

• How will you use the letterhead? Who will use it?

• What is the budget?

• How comfortable are you with taking chances? Are you a conservative company or one on the cutting edge of your business?

• Who will receive this letterhead? Who are your clients?

Know Your Client's Client

If a letterhead appeals to your clients but not to the people they need to reach, it's a failure. That's why it's important to find out everything you can about the people who will read your client's letters and pocket their business cards. Are your client's clients conservative, or do they hunger for whatever's new? Would a high-tech look intrigue them or turn them off? Will they throw away anything that looks inexpensive, or will a costly letterhead system make them think they can't afford your client? Will a humorous design solution make them laugh or make them nervous? There are infinite ways to depict any company with graphics. The "correct" way is the one that will bring your client business.

Make Certain You Can Read It

Everyone knows the frustration of hunting for a name or phone number on a letterhead. The address, phone number, fax number, and other vital information that varies with your client's business are the second most important pieces of information that any letterhead system must convey. (The first, of course, is the business name—usually presented as a logo.) Unless you can find and read this information, the letterhead is useless. That's not to say that this information must be in the top

center of the page. As the examples in this book demonstrate, the text can be in many places. And although for most applications the text should be all in one block, in some designs and for some clients it can even be scattered across the page. For some businesses, especially design firms and other creative companies, it's even appropriate to make the text difficult to read. If you know that your client's clients will take the time to decipher the necessary information, that's fine. Just be certain that your target audience has both the ability and the inclination to decipher it.

Putting a Design Together

Once you know the parameters, you can narrow the infinite design possibilities down to a few million. Sometimes, the best solution leaps out at you. But you can't count on that, so here are a few things to think about. These elements of letterhead design can be mixed in any combination. Some can be emphasized over others. But all are a part of any letterhead package.

Color: Whether your client has the budget for many colors or only one, color can be a vital part of any letterhead design. Infinite varieties of inks, including metallics and fluorescents, put an array of effects at your disposal. Remember, a one-color job doesn't have to be black. Even for the most conservative client, a dark green or purple ink might be

just the touch that sets one bank or engineering firm apart from the rest.

Type: From old standards like Garamond and Bodoni to the new electronic typefaces that seem to pop up daily, there's no end to the type families you have at your disposal. Type can express a great deal about a business—if it wasn't so expressive, there wouldn't be so many faces. Changing an existing face either electronically or by hand creates even more options. And hand lettering is an often overlooked alternative.

Paper: Too many people think only of white paper when they think of business letterhead. The variety of business papers now available can truly stagger the mind. Even the smallest print shop is likely to stock a number of unusual papers. Whether textured, colored, recycled, or coated, papers can create a variety of effects. For a project with a small budget, choosing an unusual paper or two can create a distinctive look at a low cost.

Printing: Most letterhead is printed by offset lithography, which itself offers a number of options. But there are other printing methods, each of which creates a distinctive look. Screenprinting produces thick, saturated color; letterpress produces crisp, embossed images. Die cuts, foil stamping, varnishes, and other printer's effects can make a big impact.

Logo: Often a letterhead job also includes designing or updating a company logo. Corporate identity is a discipline in itself, but in general the same rules apply: Make sure it reflects your client, appeals to your client's clients, and communicates the company name clearly and readably. While designing or redesigning a logo gives you many options in letterhead design, using an existing logo doesn't necessarily restrict your design options too much. Even an ugly or outdated logo can be successfully incorporated into a fresh design with a little ingenuity.

Artwork: Whether it's restricted to the logo or it takes up every inch of the paper, artwork gives a letterhead package style and personality. Illustrations and photography are both suitable, as is an ornamental letter or two. For budget work, clip art can provide fodder for creativity, as can scanned personal photographs. Art created directly on the page with markers, watercolors, rubber stamps or pens can personalize a pre-printed page for almost no money, though it takes a lot of work from your client.

Cost Considerations

It seems as if everyone is on a budget these days, and saving money is more important than ever. And because most large corporations have a unified graphics system that's rarely replaced, it's most likely that your letterhead projects will come from small businesses.

Whether they've got one employee or one hundred, small businesses usually don't have a lot of money for graphics, let alone for such niceties as illustration, embossing or four-color printing. Using one-color artwork and standard papers is an obvious way to keep costs down. Trading design services for printing is another time-honored way to shave expenses, but it's hardly one you can use for every project. And while computerization of such tasks as typesetting and layout at one time saved a good deal of money, they're now so common that they're usually taken for granted as part of the package.

When budget is paramount, designers often come up with creative ways to cut costs. Dozens of projects in this book—many of them in chapters other than the low-budget design chapter—were produced inexpensively. As you read their descriptions, you'll find out how.

How to Design a Winner

The projects featured here are all winners—five judges chose them from nearly eight hundred entries. But many of the others that didn't make it into this book, like thousands of entries that never make it into magazines, annuals and contests, are winners too. There's no one right solution for any design problem. But some solutions are more right than others. If you know your client and your client's client, and you make certain that your client's name, address and phone can be read and used, you'll have covered all the bases. And if you use the elements of letterhead design well, as the designers featured here have done, you too will create winning designs. In "real life," winning designs are those that do their jobs. If you

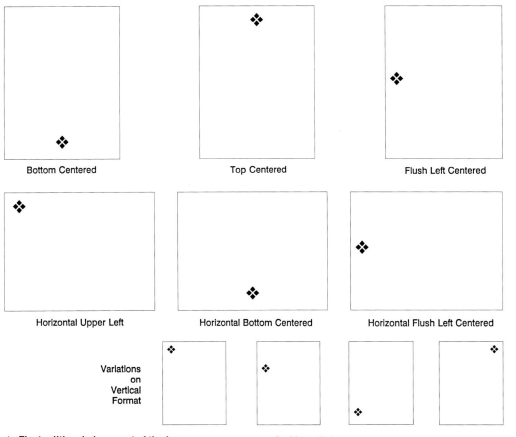

Bottom Centered   Top Centered   Flush Left Centered

Horizontal Upper Left   Horizontal Bottom Centered   Horizontal Flush Left Centered

Variations on Vertical Format

▲ The traditional placement of the logo, company name and address is in the upper-left corner of the sheet, but you can, in fact, put them just about anywhere. Let your design suggest the placement. If you are doing a strongly symmetrical design, placing the information anywhere but the top center of the sheet may throw the design off entirely. However, a design that suggests motion might call for placement in the upper left or even in the upper right. Remember that the paper is to be typed and written on. Don't let your design get in the way of communication unless there is a compelling reason to do so.

design a letterhead package that helps your client's business grow and prosper, you've won something more valuable than any trophy. And you've used your power well.

A Printing Primer

Printing techniques can be difficult to use well. Choose the wrong paper and your emboss will perforate. Specify a metallic ink when you really want a foil stamp, and you'll be disappointed. Before you try any new technique, discuss it with your printer. In the meantime, here's a quick guide to printing effects.

Some effects cost much more than others. Price depends on many variables: whether the printer has to reconfigure presses, whether special materials or papers are needed, whether extra press time is required, and what base costs run in the area. According to the National Association of Printers and Lithographers, prices are likely to be higher in large cities than they will be in smaller urban areas, regardless of what region of the country they're located in. The following price guides are estimates only.

Bleed. A bleed is a photograph or other design element that runs off one or more edges of the paper; "full bleed" artwork runs off all four edges. Incorporating bleeds can be expensive, because the printed piece must be larger than the finished piece, then trimmed to final size. This means using a larger sheet of paper for

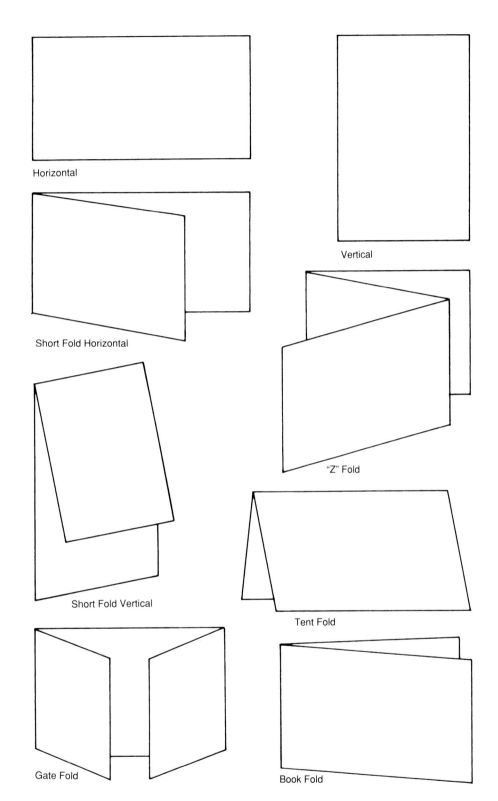

Horizontal

Vertical

Short Fold Horizontal

"Z" Fold

Short Fold Vertical

Tent Fold

Gate Fold

Book Fold

▲ **Business cards can be folded or unfolded. They can have a design or information printed on one side or both sides; the choices are virtually limitless. A business card, however, should be durable and easy to carry. Because cards are handled frequently, they should be printed on a heavy weight of paper, for example, 65# or 80# cover stock. Most business cards measure 3½ x 2 inches, but through folds and die cuts, many kinds of cards may be produced. If the business card will be folded, have it scored on the press to ensure accuracy.**

printing, which is more expensive, or printing fewer pieces per page, which means buying more paper. Cutting alone can add 20-25% to the bill. Envelopes incorporating bleed artwork are usually printed on flat stock, then cut and folded. Printing on finished envelopes also adds extra cost.

Converted envelopes. Printing the paper stock before printing and gluing ("converting") allows you to use bleeds, embosses, die cuts, and other special effects that would be impossible—or at the least, expensive—with finished envelopes.

Debossing. The opposite of embossing, debossing uses a die to create an image that's lowered rather than raised. Costs are similar; see **embossing** for details.

Die cut. Die cuts are shapes cut onto a printed piece with dies. Usually less expensive than embossing dies, cutting dies start at about $75 but can cost much more, depending on their complexity. The cutting also adds a small charge. When specifying a die cut, choose a heavy paper (at least 22 pounds) and avoid intricate patterns that could tear easily.

Double bump. A double bump or hit means running the same color twice to ensure that it's bright and clear. The cost is usually about the same as a second color.

Dry trap. Dry trapping, often used for varnishes, means printing a second color on the first after it's fully dried. It creates glossier colors and sharper edges, but is much more expensive because it requires the printer to essentially do two print jobs—requiring a new make-ready, separate press time, and additional waste sheets.

Embossing. Embossing uses heat and metal dies to produce raised type or graphics. Many effects are possible, including three-dimensional art and beveled edges. Foil can be added (see **foil stamping**) for additional effects, but blind embossing, which produces a bas-relief effect, is popular and classic. Prices vary with the complexity of the design and the depth of the emboss. Dies start at about $150 for a simple letter or shape, but can go above $1,000. Specify strong paper, and design with the emboss in mind: Allow plenty of space between printed and embossed design elements to account for the paper's movement, and keep in mind that blind embossing looks smaller once it's done than it does when designed.

Engraving. A time-honored printing method, engraving produces precise, fine lines and is ideal for small type. The process uses an etched plate, a smooth counterplate, and a special engraving press. The plate is inked, then wiped dry, so the ink adheres only to the engraved areas. You may have

to use a specialty printer. When designing for engraving, keep the following tips in mind: The smaller and more intricate your artwork, the shallower the engraving; most engraving presses use 5" x 8" plates, so letterheads with engraving at the top and bottom may require two press runs; and heavy paper (at least 20 to 24 pounds) will work best—the heavier the paper, the deeper the etch can be. Because engraving plates last a long time, they can be used for more than one printed piece, which makes engraving more affordable.

Foil stamping. Similar to embossing, this technique stamps thin foils to the paper with a hot metal die. Price varies with the complexity of the die (starting at about $100) and the type of foil used. Metallic, clear, colored, and patterned foils in various gloss or matte combinations are all available. A slightly debossed effect can be produced by stamping the foil flat. Tinted films, called foil enhancers, can also be applied to make the foils look richer or more legible.

When designing for foil stamping, keep these tips in mind: Foils can be stamped over one another; the process can discolor some papers, particularly browns, yellows and oranges; not all Pantone colors can be matched in foils; and like inks, foils can look different against different colors of paper stock. Use heavy paper, allow plenty of space between

foil stamped and printed artwork, and remember that flat foil stamps look larger once printed.

Ghosting. A ghosted effect is created by overprinting two colors at different percentages. When using a combination of dark and light inks, print the dark ink first.

Halftone. A halftone uses a screen to photographically reproduce continuous tone artwork as a series of tiny dots. Various screen patterns are available. Halftones reproduce best on smooth paper; some high-quality papers are too uneven and porous for halftones to reproduce well.

Hand coloring. Probably the most inexpensive, and most labor-intensive, way to add color to a printed piece. Hand coloring adds creativity and spontaneity, but must be done well.

Line drawing. Any black image on a white background.

Metallic inks. More expensive than colored inks, metallic inks glitter with flecks of metal (usually brass or aluminum), but are not as reflective as metal foils. The most opaque of offset inks, they print best on premium papers that don't absorb ink.

Offset lithography. The most common printing method for letterhead, offset lithography uses a metal or paper plate with a positive image photographically produced on its surface. The image attracts ink and repels water, while the rest of the plate attracts water and repels ink. The plate transfers the image to a "blanket," which then prints on the paper.

Rubber stamps. Now a popular decorative device, rubber stamps are a relatively inexpensive, though time-consuming, way to add color to a printed piece. Beginning at about $5 (but going up as high as $30 or more, depending on the complexity and size of the image), stamps can be custom-made with any image or message. Pre-made stamps of almost every description are available at stores or through catalogs. When using a pre-made stamp, however, remember that not all rubber stamp art is copyright-free; when in doubt, use a rubber stamp that has been created from your own art.

Screen tint. Like a halftone, screen tints use dot patterns to produce the desired image—in this case an even swatch of color. The density of the dots determines the strength of the color. By using several screen tints, you can create the appearance of multiple colors at a low cost.

Split fountain. By splitting a single ink fountain into sections, a printer can run several colors for the price of one. However, you must design accordingly.

Thermography. Like engraving, thermography produces a raised, rough surface. It's less expensive than engraving, but you will still need to use a specialty printer. The process involves applying a special powder to a printed sheet, then heating it until the powder melts. Type as small as four point can be used, but don't combine fine line and solid thermography on one sheet— they require different resins. Specify at least 20 pound paper.

Varnish. Either protective or decorative, varnishes come in a variety of finishes from dull to high gloss. There are two processes: spot and full-coat. Spot varnishing, usually applied over printed artwork, requires exact registration and the same make-ready work as ink printing, and is therefore similar in cost to a second color. Full-coat varnishing covers the whole page, and doesn't require a printing plate, so it's less expensive. Varnish works best on coated paper.

LOW
BUDGET

To many people, low-budget design simply means black printing on white paper. But as the following pages prove, there are many ways to get a big impact for a small price.

Some designers, of course, save printing costs by trading design for printing. While it's a time-honored solution, it's not one you can count on very often. Likewise, you can save money by printing a business card on the corner of a press sheet of a larger job, or by using the same paper and ink as another (more expensive) project.

But even when it has to be paid for in full, there are many ways to design a great low-budget piece. Distinctive paper goes a long way toward making an impression, and there are more papers than ever to choose from. Hand-coloring with markers or rubber stamps can add a second color for next to nothing, while the truly dedicated can die cut their letterhead by hand.

One extra ink color, used well, can be as effective as four-color process. And clever design can even make the old black-on-white standby something that demands notice. Like most design parameters, a small budget can force a designer to think more creatively and thus make a better product.

Designer/Studio Julie Bush/Julie Bush Designs

Client/Service Just Desserts, Stuart, FL/dessert-only catering

Paper Neenah Classic Crest, Earthstone

Type Shelly Andante (name), Copperplate (address)

Colors Two, match

Printing Offset

Software Adobe Photoshop, Adobe Illustrator

Concept Black bars, script type, textured paper and bright purple illustrations give this card—the client's primary communication piece—a memorable look for a small cost. Images of tumbling kitchen equipment make a light-hearted reference to desserts, the client's specialty.

Cost-Saving Techniques The designer waived her design fee and used copyright-free clip art to save illustration charges, then output the type with another job. To cut printing costs, the cards were quick-printed.

Cost $93   **Print Run** 500

Art Director/Studio Joven Orozzo/Joven Orozzo Design

Designer/Studio Joven Orozzo/Joven Orozzo Design

Client/Service David Millar Ltd./film editing

Paper Transparency film

Type Futura

Color One, black

Printing Photocopying

Software Adobe Illustrator

Concept This card represents its owner's business more literally than most cards ever can. Printed on transparency plastic, the hand-cut cards look and feel like film, leaving no need for anything but the client's name and telephone number. The graphic slash above the client's name symbolizes editing.

Special Production Technique Printing was too expensive for a print run of 150, so the designer used a Cannon copier to print the cards on film, then cut them out by hand.

Print Run 150

Designer/Studio Thomas Scott/Eye Noise

Client/Service Eye Noise, Orlando, FL/graphic design

Paper Fox River Circa Select, Moss Recycled

Type Franklin Gothic Book, Heavy and Heavy Oblique

Colors Two, match

Printing Offset

Software Adobe Illustrator, Adobe Photoshop

Concept A business card-sized booklet, humorously describing a designer's work in words and pictures, serves as a memorable introduction to new clients. Most images are found objects that the designer scanned on his flatbed scanner. According to the designer, while not everyone gets the jokes on the card, most people do keep and remember it.

Cost-Saving Techniques The designer used a corner of a press sheet from a client's job. The printer output the film, trimmed the piece and scored the pages at no cost, and the designer collated and stapled the pages himself.

Cost $0 **Print Run** 1,000

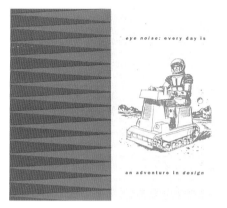

Art Director/Studio Lewis Glaser/Wet Paper Bag Graphic Design
Designer/Studio Lewis Glaser/Wet Paper Bag Graphic Design
Client/Service Thad A. Duhigg, Fort Worth, TX/sculptor in steel
Paper Simpson Quest, White
Type Industria, ITC Kabel Family
Color One, black, plus hand-coloring
Printing Offset
Software Adobe Illustrator, Adobe Streamline, QuarkXPress

Concept Much of the sculptor's work is in welded steel. Simple type, a striking image of a welder, and rugged paper combine to achieve a humorous industrial look. The result, according to the designer, is unusually appealing to fine artists and has been well received by the sculptor's clients.
Cost-Saving Technique The hand-colored yellow welding flash adds spontaneity and intensity as well as a second color.
Cost $1,000 **Print Run** 500

Thad A. Duhigg / Sculpture that Works / 2367 Park Place / Fort Worth, Texas 76110 / 817.922.9725

Thad A. Duhigg
Sculpture that Works
2367 Park Place
Fort Worth, Texas 76110
817.922.9725

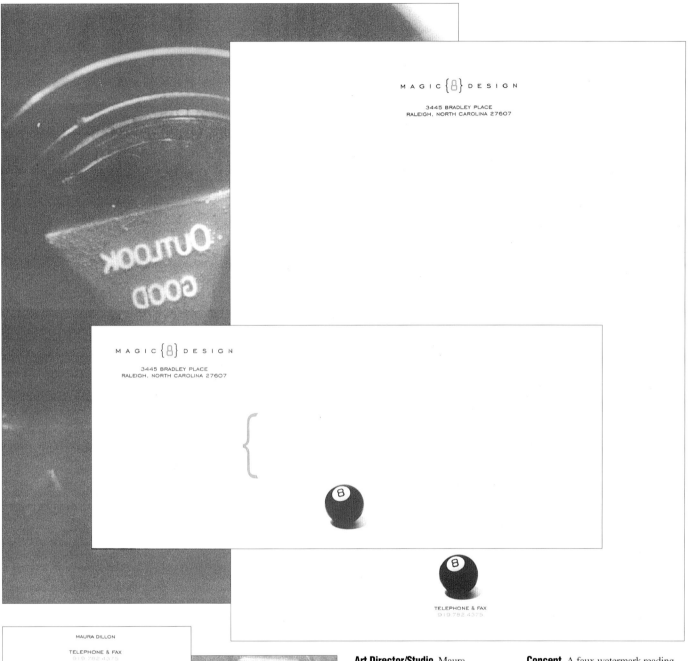

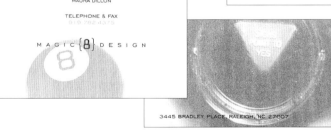

Art Director/Studio Maura Dillon/Magic {8} Design

Designer/Studio Maura Dillon/Magic {8} Design

Client/Service Magic {8} Design, Raleigh, NC/graphic design

Photographers Lee Moore, Brady McNamara

Paper Gilbert ESSE Whitegreen, smooth and textured

Type Engravers Gothic, BT Regular

Colors Two, match

Printing Offset

Software Aldus FreeHand, Adobe Photoshop

Concept A faux watermark reading "Outlook good" (a result of printing a photograph of the familiar Magic 8-ball toy on the back of the letterhead) helped the designer create a clever, memorable letterhead. The clean design and sophisticated color scheme keeps the package from succumbing to kitsch, while the playful name and photographs keep it from appearing stiff.

Cost $1,260   **Print Run** 1,000

Art Director/Studio Barbara Taff/Potomac Communications
Designer/Studio Barbara Taff/Potomac Communications
Illustrator William Brown
Client/Service Potomac Communications, Washington, DC/graphic design and communications
Paper Neenah Environment, Woodstock
Type Stempel Garamond Old Style
Colors Two, match
Printing Offset
Software QuarkXPress

Concept The old-style type and woodcut-style illustrations refer both to the design firm's name and to the quality its owner wanted to stress: permanence. The use of dull red and dark gray, rather than simple red and black, give this letterhead a sense of dignity and distinction that belie its price tag.
Cost $615   **Print Run** 1,000

POTOMAC COMMUNICATIONS

BARBARA O. TAFF
PRESIDENT

3925 JENIFER STREET, N.W.
WASHINGTON, D.C. 20015

TEL 202 362 5933
FAX 202 362 5841

POTOMAC COMMUNICATIONS

BARBARA O. TAFF
PRESIDENT

3925 JENIFER STREET, N.W.
WASHINGTON, D.C. 20015

TEL 202 362 5933
FAX 202 362 5841

POTOMAC COMMUNICATIONS

STEVEN TRANK PHOTOGRAPHY

Art Director/Studio Carrie Brazell/Brazell Design
Designers/Studio Carrie Brazell, Jerry Roethig/Brazell Design
Photographer Steven Trank
Client/Service Steven Trank Photography, Columbus, OH/photography
Paper Gilbert Neu-tech Ultra, White Wove; polystyrene (card)
Type Copperplate (name), Times Roman (address)
Colors Two, match
Printing Offset
Software QuarkXPress, Adobe Photoshop

Concept Contemporary colors, a two-color blend and classic type work with a photographer's F-stop scale and a photograph of a cable release to create an unusual design that communicates the client's business. Translucent business cards add a memorable touch.
Cost $1,500 **Print Run** 2,000

STEVEN TRANK PHOTOGRAPHY

780 King Avenue
Columbus, Ohio 43212
Phone and Fax:
614·299·8400

780 King Avenue
Columbus, Ohio 43212

780 King Avenue
Columbus,
Ohio 43212

Phone and Fax
614-299-8400

STEVEN TRANK PHOTOGRAPHY

Art Director/Studio Mara
Hines/Mara Hines Graphic Design
Designer/Studio Mara Hines/Mara
Hines Graphic Design
Client/Service Mara Hines Graphic
Design, Marshfield Hills, MA/graph-
ic design
Paper Neenah Environment,
Moonrock
Type Frugal Sans (name and
address), Copperplate (logo),
Garamond (name)
Colors Two, match
Printing Offset
Software Aldus FreeHand, Aldus
PageMaker

Concept An unusual shade of orange
ink, the computer-modified image,
and the distinctive use of type reflect
the designer's sense of style: modern
and slightly off-beat. The black bar
bordering the letterhead and card
make a strong statement, helping the
designer's correspondence to stand
out on her clients' desks—especially
helpful for her proposals and invoices.
Cost $400

Art Director/Studio Art
Garcia/SullivanPerkins
Designer/Studio Art
Garcia/SullivanPerkins
Client/Service David Hernandez,
Chicago, IL/auto repair
Paper Strathmore Renewal
Type Rockwall
Color One, black
Printing Offset
Software QuarkXPress

Concept Wit and the use of an
intriguing paper set this package apart
from other one-color letterheads.
Fingerprints—a visual touch synony-
mous with mechanics—seem to dirty
the otherwise plain stationery; with
this clever touch the client leaves a
lasting impression.

Special Production Technique
Fingerprints were positioned directly
on the mechanical and were shot as
halftones.

Print Run 1,000

Art Directors/Studio David Covell, Michael Jager/Jager Di Paola Kemp Design

Designer/Studio David Covell/Jager Di Paola Kemp Design

Client/Service Jager Di Paola Kemp Design, Burlington, VT/graphic design

Paper Crane's Crest (letterhead), Curtis Tuscan Antique (cards)

Type Din, News Gothic

Colors Four, match

Printing Offset

Software Aldus FreeHand

Concept A new identity for a maturing design firm called for letterhead exuding confidence and style, as well as one that could be adapted for many print uses. The firm chose classic colors and design elements, combining them in a contemporary layout to show its respect for both the past and the present. Sans serif type and blocks of saturated color create an industrial look and inspire trust.

Cost $4,396 **Print Run** 6,950 (letterhead), 10,000 (cards)

ESCAPE

FAMILY
RESOURCE
CENTER

3210 Eastside
Houston, TX 77098
Tel: (713) 942-9500
Fax: (713) 942-0702

FOUNDED BY
THE NATIONAL
EXCHANGE CLUB

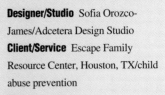

Designer/Studio Sofia Orozco-James/Adcetera Design Studio
Client/Service Escape Family Resource Center, Houston, TX/child abuse prevention
Type Baker Signet
Color One, match
Printing Offset

Concept An unusual ink color, an impressionist illustration, and a distinctive lean typeface give this simple package dignity and elegance. The designer placed the logotype of the organization's founder in the lower right-hand corner, where it complements the design rather than competes with it.
Print Run 5,000

ESCAPE

Glynis Grief
PARENT AIDE SUPERVISOR

FAMILY
RESOURCE
CENTER

3210 Eastside
Houston, TX 77098
Tel: (713) 942-9500
Fax: (713) 942-0702

ESCAPE

FAMILY
RESOURCE
CENTER

3210 Eastside
Houston, TX 77098

Quoi de Neuf? communication

3315 France Prime suite 713
Ste-Foy, Québec
G1W 4X3

Quoi de Neuf? communication

3315 France Prime suite 713   **Nicolas Pedneault,** B.A.V.
Ste-Foy, Québec   concepteur visuel
G1W 4X3

Tél: 418 658 3731
Fax: 418 653 4986

Quoi de Neuf? communication

3315 France Prime suite 713
Ste-Foy, Québec
G1W 4X3

Tél: 418 658 3731
Fax: 418 653 4986

Art Director/Studio Nicolas
Pedneault/Quoi de Neuf?
Communication
Designer/Studio Nicolas
Pedneault/Quoi de Neuf?
Communication
Client/Service Quoi de Neuf?
Communication, Ste-Foy, Quebec,
Canada/communications
Paper Fox River Confetti, tan
Type Frutiger
Color One plus varnish
Printing Offset
Software QuarkXPress

Concept Dark textured paper, further
darkened by a varnish, gives this letterhead a distinctive look at first
glance. The designer used a screen of
black for the shadow on the running
figure and two weights of the project
typeface to create the illusion of two
colors. The unvarnished question
mark, quotation marks and circle at
the center of each piece add more
visual interest.
Cost $600 (Canadian)
Print Run 1,000

Anne Semmes

FOOD CONSULTANT

Anne Semmes

FOOD CONSULTANT

55 Cambridge Drive ❧ Short Hills, NJ 07078 ❧ 201.376.5595

Art Director/Studio Toni
Schowalter/Schowalter 2 Design
Designer/Studio Ilene
Price/Schowalter 2 Design
Client/Service Anne Semmes, Short
Hills, NJ/food consultant
Paper Strathmore Writing, Natural
White
Type Gravure (name), Garamond #3
(address), Zapf Dingbats
Color One, match
Printing Offset
Software QuarkXPress

Concept The conservative client
wanted a witty design to set her apart
without appearing frivolous. The
package combines elegance—classic
green on cream, timeless typefaces,
and artwork with the look of a nine-
teenth century engraving—with sly
humor.
Cost $800   **Print Run** 1,000

55 Cambridge Drive ❧ Short Hills, New Jersey 07078 ❧ 201.376.5595

Anne Semmes

FOOD CONSULTANT

55 Cambridge Drive ❧ Short Hills, New Jersey 07078

Designer Carolyn Brown
Client/Service Carlos O'Connor,
Rahway, NJ/Mexican restaurant
Paper Simpson Quest, Moss
Type Hand-lettering
Colors Two, match
Printing Screen printing

Concept To reflect the spirit of
Carlos O'Connor, a restaurant with
an eclectic mix of Irish music and
decor with Mexican food, the designer echoes this unexpected combination in her design for this letterhead
package. The logo, a cactus sham-
rock, sets the eclectic tone. A sprinkling of cactus needles, printed in a
green only slightly darker than the
paper, enliven the pieces; a fold-out
business card creates further interest.
Cost-Saving Technique Screen printing gives the piece its rich color,
while allowing the letterhead to be
printed in small quantities.
Cost $500 **Print Run** 250

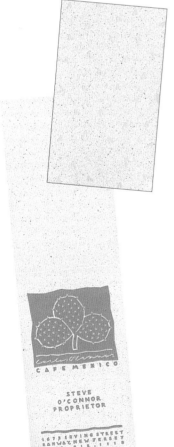

1. What is Trudy Cole-Zielanski?
   ❑ a graphic designer
   ❑ an educator
   ❑ all of the above
   ❑ none of the above

2. Where is TCZ?
   ❑ Rt1 Box 362
      Mount Solon, VA 22843
   ❑ M114 Duke Hall
      James Madison University
      Harrisonburg, VA 22807
   ❑ all of the above
   ❑ none of the above

3. How can she be reached?
   ❑ by phone at 703-568-3488
   ❑ by phone at 703-350-2011
   ❑ by e-mail at
      IN%"FAC_TCOLEZIE
      @VAX2.ACS.JMU.EDU"
   ❑ all of the above
   ❑ none of the above

Score: _____

Designer/Studio Trudy Cole-Zielanski/Trudy Cole-Zielanski Design
Client/Studio Trudy Cole-Zielanski Design, Mt. Solon, VA/graphic design
Color One, black
Printing Offset
Software Adobe Illustrator, QuarkXPress

Concept The playful design of this piece sets it far apart from the slick letterheads of most design firms. Cole-Zielanski, both a teacher and a designer, disguised her letterhead— the stationery as a test, the card as a page of a textbook, the envelope (complete with die-cut circles) as inter-office mail. The result is a set that effectively communicates both her personality and her position.
Cost $750 **Print Run** 500

, Logos
ochures
llustra-
rations,
posters,
rs, con-
ncepts,
position
ments,
rs cata-
g u e s
s, mail-
rheads

been published in national and international graphic design annuals. troubleshooter; problem solver; illustrator, etc. [Colloq.]
Trú'dy Çōle-Zië'lan·şkï *n. Pol. pers. f.* 1. (a) a graphic designer, as in *Trudy Cole-Zielansk Design* (b) an educator; associate prof. of graphic design 2. resident of Rte 1 box 362 Moun Solon, VA 22843-9607, phone 703-568-3488 3 inhabitant of Duke Hall M114, The School o Media Arts & Design, James Madison University, Harrisonburg, VA 22807, phone 703-350-2011 or 703-568-6216 4. E-mailer a IN%" FAC_TCOLEZIE@VAX2.ACS.JMU.EDU

Art Director/Studio Earl Gee/Earl
Gee Design
Designer/Studio Earl Gee/Earl Gee
Design
Client/Service Daven Film & Video,
San Francisco, CA/production house
Paper French Speckletone Natural
cover and text
Type Futura Medium and Extra Bold
Colors Two, match
Printing Offset
Software QuarkXPress, Adobe
Illustrator

Concept The mixture of letters and
film-related icons represent the eclectic nature of the client's work and
also symbolizes its creative approach
to projects. A fold-out business card
adds to the visual impact. The client
adapted the icon system to an animated introduction for its demo film.
Cost $1,573.28 **Print Run** 1,000

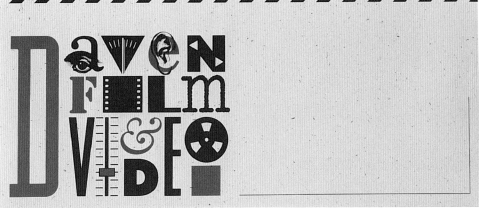

Architecture + Development

T R I U M P H

Art Director/Studio Maureen Erbe/
Maureen Erbe Design
Designers/Studio Rita A. Sowins,
Maureen Erbe/Maureen Erbe Design
Client/Service Triumph Design, Los
Angeles, CA/architecture, construc-
tion and development
Paper French Speckletone Madero
Beach text and cover
Type Belucian, Triplex, Raleigh
Gothic, Futura Condensed
Colors Three, match
Printing Letterpress
Software QuarkXPress

Concept The elegance of letterpress
combines with lean, spare type and a
sophisticated color scheme to convey
the client's desired image: creative
and tasteful. Recycled paper stock
adds to the creative feel without sac-
rificing professionalism.
Special Visual Effect The imagery at
the top was taken from a detail of one
of the client's architectural projects.
Cost-Saving Technique The package
was printed at the same time as two
other letterhead packages using the
same paper stock and ink.
Cost $670 **Print Run** 500

TRIUMPH DESIGN + DEVELOPMENT

1912 CREST DRIVE, LOS ANGELES, CA 90034

TELEPHONE: (310) 558-0957

CALIFORNIA 90034

LOS ANGELES

1912 CREST DRIVE

Architecture + Construction + Development

T R I U M P H

Architecture + Development

T R I U M P H

T R I U M P H

DOUGLAS K. HENDRON
A I A

TRIUMPH
DESIGN + DEVELOPMENT
1912 CREST DRIVE
LOS ANGELES, CA 90034

Fax: (310) 841-6097

TELEPHONE:
(310) 558-0957

Designer/Studio Beth Carlisle/Susan Smith Illustration
Illustrator Susan Smith
Client/Service Susan Smith, Boston, MA/illustration
Paper Strathmore Writing
Type Hand-lettering
Colors Four, process
Printing Offset

Concept Hand-lettering and tiny illustrations introduce the illustrator's style without the expense of a formal promotion. The four-color drawings were chosen to appeal to designers, in the hope that the package will encourage art directors to think of illustration as part of a design format.
Cost-Saving Technique The designer traded illustration for printing.
Cost $500   **Print Run** 6,000

Art Director/Studio Darryl
Brown/Miller Brooks Inc.
Designer/Studio Darryl
Brown/Miller Brooks Inc.
Client/Service Christine Gentry,
Indianapolis, IN/space designer, film
stylist and artist
Paper French Dur-o-tone, Butcher
Off-White (letterhead); brown kraft
(envelope); Dur-o-tone Packing
Carton (business card)
Type Orator, Franklin Gothic
Colors Three, match (two per piece)
Printing Offset
Software QuarkXPress, Adobe
Photoshop, Adobe Illustrator

Concept The client's diverse audience of art directors, art buyers, and
business owners all share one quality:
They like unusual design. The package's textured papers and square type
give it an industrial look that con-
trasts with the organic decorative elements. This juxtaposition reflects the
client's style of commercial work and
fine art.
Cost-Saving Techniques A start-up
printer used this package to test its
presses, donating the work. In defer-
ence to the donation, the designer
kept each piece to two colors.
Cost $0   **Print Run** 1,500

ART DIRECTION

COMPUTER DESIGN

COMPUTER ILLUSTRATION

CORPORATE IDENTITY

BROCHURES

GRAPHIC COMMUNICATIONS

PACKAGING

PROMOTIONAL MATERIAL

SIGNAGE/DISPLAY

(ETCETERA)

206/255-5809
fax 206/226-5765

Post Office Box 454
Issaquah, Wash 98027

Designer/Studio Robert M. Brünz/RM Brünz Studio
Client/Service RM Brünz Studio, Issaquah, WA/graphic design
Paper Simpson Protocol, Bright White
Type Cabarga Cursiva (name), Futura
Colors Four, process
Printing Offset
Software Aldus FreeHand

Concept The heroic, WPA-style graphic was designed to convey the quality of the designer's work, while the letterhead lists the firm's diverse services. The four-color card, die-cut and scored, makes a strong impression and serves as a keepsake for clients.

Special Visual Effect To keep his business card on client desktops, Brünz wanted a stand-alone card. However, he found that many clients disliked similar cards that couldn't be stored traditionally. By designing a card that folds to traditional size, he ensured that clients who didn't keep his card out wouldn't discard it in frustration.

Cost $1,400   **Print Run** 4,000

Art Director/Studio Cindy Wrobel/Cindy Wrobel Design & Illustration

Designer/Studio Cindy Wrobel/Cindy Wrobel Design & Illustration

Client/Service Cindy Wrobel, St. Louis, MO/design and illustration

Paper Beckett Cambric Writing (letterhead package), Strathmore Writing (label)

Type Piegnot

Colors Two, match

Printing Offset

Concept Bold two-color printing and a graphic that takes up most of the space, even on the letterhead, immediately distinguishes this colorful package. The designer updated her logo, a palette and triangle, by rendering it in the popular scratchboard style. A screen of the design on the stationery sheet ensures that letters will still be easy to read.

Special Production Technique To match the letterhead while using available label stock, the printer made a line shot of the textured paper stock and printed it in purple on the plain white labels.

Cost $1,500   **Print Run** 2,000 (letterhead and cards), 1,000 (envelopes), 500 (labels)

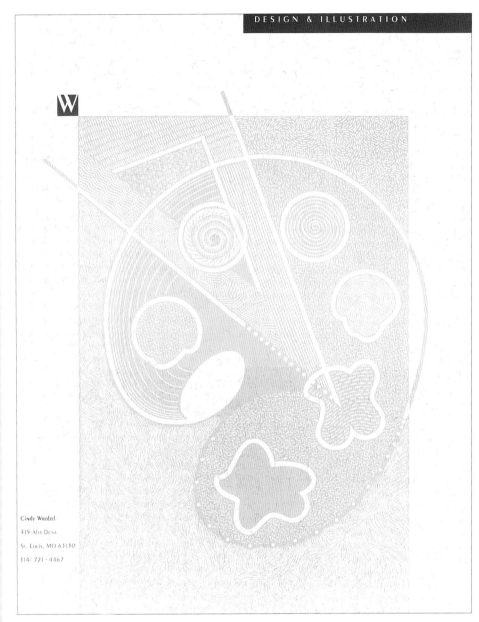

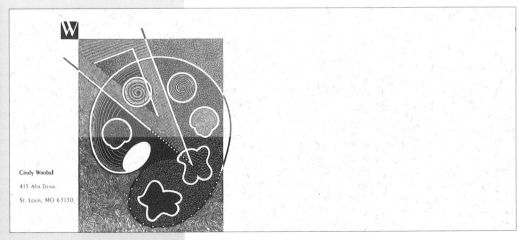

Art Director/Studio Evan A. Schultz/Armstrong Creative
Designer/Studio Evan A. Schultz/Armstrong Creative
Client/Service William Nahn, Madison, WI/copywriting, radio/television production
Paper Champion Kromekote 2000 Enamel, Avon Brilliant White Classic Crest
Type Caslon 540
Color One, black
Printing Offset
Software Adobe Photoshop, QuarkXPress
Concept To attract clients interested in diverse, lively film work, the designer played on the name of the client's business, mixing the letters of the name to show that the client made sense of nonsense. They also emphasized Nahn's symbol, a combination comma and exclamation point that symbolizes the film editor's desire to make new marks in writing. Creative use of type on the business card and a distinctive vellum letterhead further distinguish this inexpensive package.
Special Production Technique To print the logo in reverse on the back of the vellum paper, the negatives were used backwards, emulsion side up.
Cost $150   **Print Run** 500

Art Director/Studio Laura Quinlivan/Riddell Advertising & Design

Designer/Studio Laura Quinlivan/Riddell Advertising & Design

Client/Service Riddell Advertising & Design, Jackson Hole, WY/advertising and design

Paper Simpson EverGreen, Aspen

Type Copperplate

Colors Six, match

Printing Offset

Software QuarkXPress, Adobe Photoshop

Concept Because of this studio's location in Jackson Hole, Wyoming, moose and bison are as much a part of the designer's day-to-day world as clients and concepts, and the designer wanted this piece to reflect that. Bright blocks of color and exceptionally readable type communicate the sophisticated yet friendly spirit of this studio. Copyright-free engravings provide the illustrations for this package, which includes three different designs.

Special Production Technique The inside of the converted envelopes are printed with the same Toyo ink used in the rest of the design.

Cost $2,625   **Print Run** 7,500

Art Director/Studio Bryan L. Peterson/Peterson & Company

Designer/Studio Bryan L. Peterson/Peterson & Company

Photography John Wong Photography

Client/Service InfoFusion/college marketing and strategies

Paper Champion Benefit

Type Insignia, Courier

Colors Three, match

Printing Offset

Software Adobe Photoshop, QuarkXPress

Concept The designer is a partner in this company, a college marketing and strategy company that combines three disciplines. The letterhead explains the business and introduces all three partners, who are identified by name and number. Two ink colors (red and opaque white) and type-writer-style text in black blend well with the paper stock's unusual ochre color. The graphic—a photograph of a miniature column used for a plant stand in the photgrapher's studio—represents the business's institutional nature.

Cost-Saving Technique The project was designed to be printed on a small A B Dick press, rather than a larger, more expensive press.

Cost $1,500 **Print Run** 2,000

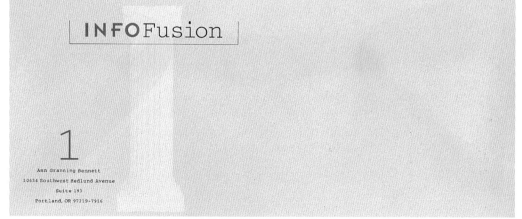

ALL MEDIA
MATERIEL
INC. FINE & GRAPHIC
ART SUPPLY

417 E. Main Street
Kent, Ohio 44240

Art Director/Studio Janice
Troutman-Rains/Troutman-Rains
Design
Designer/Studio Janice Troutman-
Rains/Troutman-Rains Design
Client/Service All Media Materiel
Inc., Kent, OH/art and graphic supply
store
Paper Simpson EverGreen, Birch
Type Optima
Color One, black plus hand-stamping
Printing Offset, rubber stamping
Software QuarkXPress

Concept This retailer needed a contemporary design to reflect its product mix, without focusing on one
design profession. The use of rubber
stamps bearing a variety of images
reflects the variety of the store's customers, creates an economical way to
achieve a second color, and gives
each piece a unique hand-done look.
Cost-Saving Technique During slow
hours, store employees decorate the
pieces with rubber stamps. Different
images and ink pads allow the store
owners to target various audiences.
Cost $550   **Print Run** 2,500

ALL MEDIA
MATERIEL
INC. FINE & GRAPHIC
ART SUPPLY

DISCOUNT CARD

ALL MEDIA
MATERIEL
INC. FINE & GRAPHIC
ART SUPPLY

417 E. Main Street
Kent, Ohio 44240
216-678-8078
Open 7 days a week

10% off all applicable purchases
must present at time of purchase

417 E. Main Street
Kent, Ohio 44240
216-678-8078

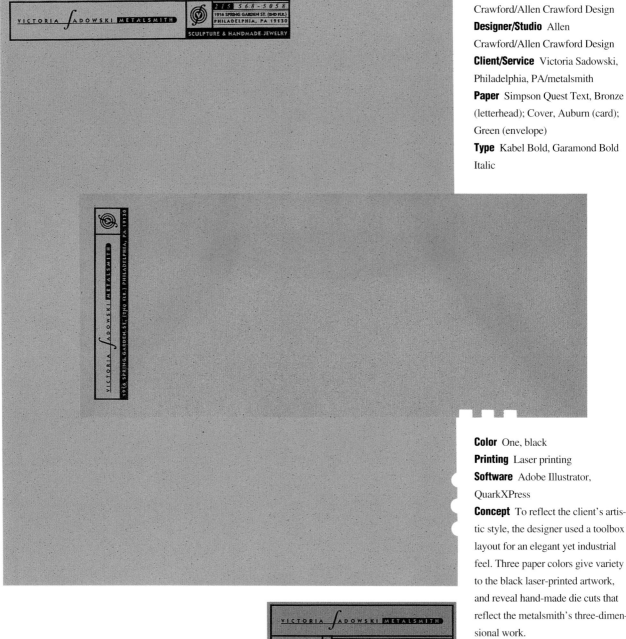

Art Director/Studio Allen Crawford/Allen Crawford Design
Designer/Studio Allen Crawford/Allen Crawford Design
Client/Service Victoria Sadowski, Philadelphia, PA/metalsmith
Paper Simpson Quest Text, Bronze (letterhead); Cover, Auburn (card); Green (envelope)
Type Kabel Bold, Garamond Bold Italic

Color One, black
Printing Laser printing
Software Adobe Illustrator, QuarkXPress
Concept To reflect the client's artistic style, the designer used a toolbox layout for an elegant yet industrial feel. Three paper colors give variety to the black laser-printed artwork, and reveal hand-made die cuts that reflect the metalsmith's three-dimensional work.
Cost-Saving Techniques The client prints her stationery as needed from her computer—a practical as well as inexpensive ploy, since she changes address frequently; die cuts are made by hand.
Cost $300

Art Director/Studio Robert L.
Peters/Circle Design Inc.
Designer/Studio Andrea
Pauch/Circle Design Inc.
Client/Service Grandmaison
Photography, Winnipeg, Manitoba,
Canada/photography
Paper Neenah Classic Crest,
Potomac Blue, cover (cards) and
writing (letterhead)
Type Akzidenz Grotesk
Color One, black
Printing Offset
Software Adobe Photoshop,
QuarkXPress

Concept To communicate the photographer's environmental work, the
designer scanned contact prints of her
client's photographs and rendered
them as shadows, making a subtle
reference to light. Two weights of
type also play on the idea of light and
shadow. A faintly metallic ink gives
the package a quiet distinction.
Special Production Techniques All
items were run together to save printing costs. To continue the feather
image to the back of the envelopes,
the printers ran them with the flaps
open.
Cost $1,750 (Canadian)
Print Run 500

Client Hotline ℂ 314 I 421-5646

611 North Tenth   Seventh Floor   Saint Louis Missouri 63101   314 I 421-0805 FAX I 421-5647

Phoenix Creative

Steve Springmeyer

Phoenix Creative
611 North Tenth
Seventh Floor
President   Saint Louis
Missouri 63101
ℂ 314 I 421-5646
FAX I 421-5647

Designers/Studio Eric Thoelke, Ed Mantels-Seeker/Phoenix Creative
Client/Service Phoenix Creative, St. Louis, MO/graphic design
Paper Mohawk Superfine (letterhead, envelope), Champion Kromekote C2S cover (business card)
Type Franklin Gothic, Meta, hand-lettering
Colors Three, match
Printing Offset
Software Aldus FreeHand

Concept The letterhead was designed to appeal to two distinct groups: corporate clients, who often prefer traditional design, and sales promotion clients, who enjoy a more playful style. The careful use of bright red and curved type hits that knife edge between the two, for a creative but responsible look.
Special Production Techniques A double pass of red on all items and gloss varnish on the red side of the business cards ensure that the color gets maximum impact. Film for the project was generated for the printer in-house.
Cost $10,000   **Print Run** 10,000

Art Director/Studio Rick Sealock/Rick Sealock Illustration

Designer/Studio Rick Sealock/Rick Sealock Illustration

Illustrator Rick Sealock

Client/Service Rick Sealock, Calgary, Alberta, Canada/illustration

Paper Beckett Cambric, Birch (letterhead and cards); kraft (envelope)

Type Clarendon Bold, Univers 67, Helvetica Antique, Grotesque 216, Clearface Heavy, American Typewriter

Color One, black

Printing Offset

Concept Accordion-folded business cards and oversized envelopes allow the illustrator to demonstrate his unique, quirky style. The letterhead package is the first part of an extended promotional campaign that includes postcards and brochures.

Special Production Technique Sealock arranged photocopies of his illustrations and Letraset type on paper for a hands-on look, rather than generating his designs on a computer.

Cost $300   **Print Run** 1,250

Art Director/Studio Dino Paul/After Hours Creative
Designers/Studio Dino Paul, Brad Smith, Todd Fedell/After Hours Creative
Photographer Kevin Cruff
Client/Service After Hours Creative, Phoenix, AZ/graphic design
Paper Gilbert Oxford
Type Futura
Colors Two, match
Printing Offset
Software Adobe Illustrator

Concept This package initially presents a classic, spare face to clients, then surprises them with a hidden full-bleed photo on the reverse side. The image, a photomontage of clock faces, interprets the studio's name and its commitment to work "after hours" to get the job done. The second color, red, is used sparingly but to maximum effect.

Special Production Technique Despite its unique look, the envelope is not custom: The designers used an existing die, but printed on the inside and left the envelopes unfinished.

Cost $3,500 **Print Run** 5,000 (letterhead, envelopes, labels, stickers), 2,500 (business cards)

CONTINENTAL MILLS, INC.
Mailing Address • P.O. Box 88176, Seattle, Washington 98138 • 206/872-8400
Shipping Address • 7186 South 192nd Street, Kent, Washington 98032 • 800/457-7744

Art Director/Studio Wendy
Harman/RM Brünz Studio
Designer/Studio Robert M.
Brünz/RM Brünz Studio
Client/Product Continental Mills,
Seattle, WA/food service products
Paper Cross Pointe Genesis, Husk
Type Garamond
Colors Four, process
Printing Offset
Software Corel Draw

Concept The designer revamped this
client's existing logo for Krusteaz
bread, adding an oval ribbon and
three heads of wheat for a nostalgic
look, then used it in a contemporary
way. The mix of a clean layout, four-
color printing, and textured paper
recalling wheat flour communicates
the client's main message: quality
and home-style goodness.
Cost $4,276   **Print Run** 20,000

CONTINENTAL MILLS, INC.
P.O. Box 88176
Seattle, Washington 98138

♻
Please recycle

Art Directors/Studio Shawn
Freeman, Todd Hart/Focus 2
Designers/Studio Shawn Freeman,
Todd Hart/Focus 2
Client/Service Focus 2, Dallas,
TX/graphic design
Paper Gilbert ESSE
Type Matrix
Colors Two, match
Printing Offset
Software QuarkXPress, Aldus
FreeHand

Concept The use of unusual layouts
and textured paper gives this letterhead a distinct feel that helps differentiate it from other mail. The pictogram, and eye with the number 2 as
a pupil, refers to the design firm's
name and contributes to the contemporary, uncluttered look of this package. The studio's contractual policies
are printed on the back of the letterhead—a smart and effective way to
reiterate these policies to clients.
Cost $600 **Print Run** 2,000

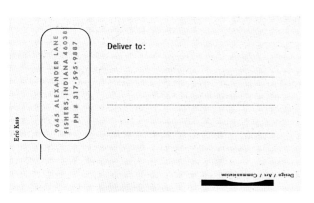

Deliver to:

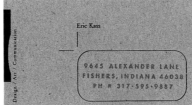

Eric Kass

9645 ALEXANDER LANE
FISHERS, INDIANA 46038
PH # 317·595·9887

Eric Kass

9645 ALEXANDER LANE
FISHERS, INDIANA 46038
PH # 317·595·9887

Art Director/Studio Eric Kass/Eric Kass Design
Designer/Studio Eric Kass/Eric Kass Design
Client/Service Eric Kass Design, Fishers, IN/graphic design
Paper French Speckletone, Chipboard (card); French Durotone, Newsprint White (letterhead); kraft (envelope)
Type Stemple Garamond (name), Futura Heavy (address)
Color One, black plus hand-stamping
Printing Offset, rubber stamping
Software Adobe Illustrator, QuarkXPress

Concept Simple brown-toned papers communicate the designer's no-nonsense attitude toward business, while creative use of black line art adds a distinctive, creative touch.
Cost-Saving Techniques One-color printing was donated. Besides adding a second color, the $15, self-inking rubber stamp used for the studio address contributes to the designer's image: classic industrial-style type applied by hand.
Cost $100 (printing donated)
Print Run 1,000

Art Director/Studio Barbara Ferguson/Barbara Ferguson Designs
Designer/Studio Barbara Ferguson/Barbara Ferguson Designs
Client/Service Barbara Ferguson Designs, Santee, CA/graphic consultation for zoological society museums
Paper Neenah Classic Crest, Millstone
Type Copperplate Heavy
Colors Two, match
Printing Offset

Concept The second color and unusual paper make a distinctive first impression, while the four illustrations demonstrate the designer's unique style in the specialized field of animal illustration. The stationery and envelopes serve as an instant portfolio, while the four different card designs have worked overtime to earn clients' notice: At initial meetings, clients are offered their choice of business card designs, which serves as a great icebreaker.
Cost $216.25 **Print Run** 750

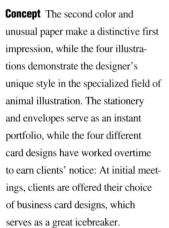

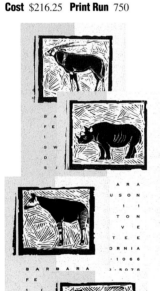

Art Director/Studio Shawn Freeman/
Focus 2
Designer/Studio Shawn Freeman/
Focus 2
Client/Service Coffee Express,
Midland, TX/mail order coffee
company
Paper French Speckletone
Type Torino
Color One, match
Printing Offset
Software QuarkXPress, Aldus
FreeHand

Concept For this gourmet coffee
seller on a tight budget, the designer
found an inexpensive printer and
chose brown-red ink and a coffee-
colored paper with a handmade look
and texture. The fine-lined logo has a
nostalgic look and features a pony
express rider, reflecting the name. A
subtly humorous addition is the use
of coffee beans as dingbats in the
logo.
Cost $150 **Print Run** 1,000

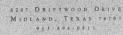

Art Director/Studio Clifford Stoltze/Stoltze Design

Designer/Studio Clifford Stoltze/Stoltze Design

Client/Service Stoltze Design, Boston, MA/graphic design

Paper Gilbert ESSE Text, White Grey Smooth

Type New Baskerville, Monotype Grotesque Black

Colors Two, match

Printing Offset

Software Aldus FreeHand

Concept The unusual color choice in ink and paper complements the designer's signature use of typography and texture. The registration mark in the contemporary logotype also recalls a target, suggesting that the firm's designs are on target.

Cost $4,000 **Print Run** 5,000 (letterhead and card), 2,000 (second sheet)

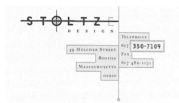

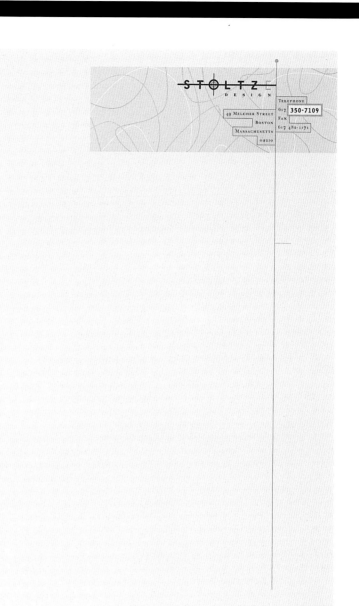

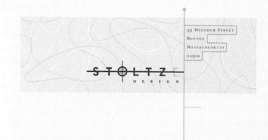

Designer/Studio Magdalena Dukeland/Half Moon Design Co.

Client/Service Firehole Photographic Expeditions, Jackson Hole, WY/photographic expeditions

Paper French Speckletone, kraft, cover and text

Type Caslon Antique

Color One, black

Printing Offset

Software QuarkXPress, Adobe Photoshop

Concept The time-honored technique of using both a full-strength color and a screen creates the look of two colors on this unusual one-color package. Caslon Antique, often a gimmicky face, fits the adventurous nature of the client's work. The dark brown paper and the use of line art, rather than photography, further differentiate this rustic package from the slick look many photographers favor.

Cost $2,000   **Print Run** 3,000

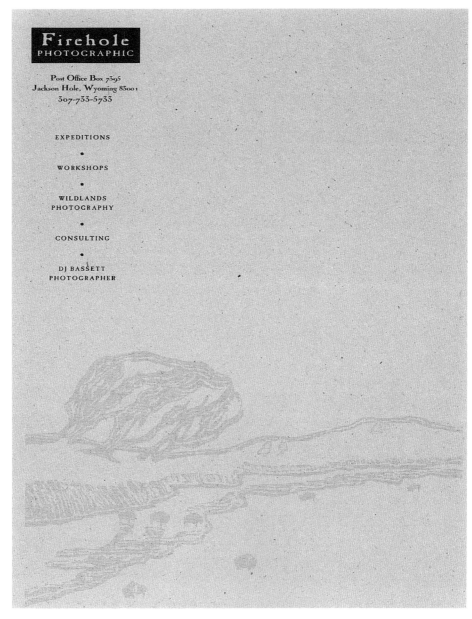

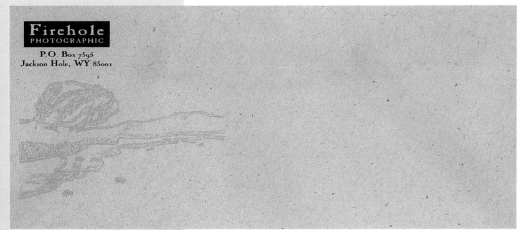

Art Director/Studio Bryan L.
Peterson/Peterson & Co.
Designer/Studio Bryan L.
Peterson/Peterson & Co.
Client/Service John Wong
Photography, Dallas, TX/photography
Paper Crane Classic Crest
Type OG Gothic No. 3
Colors Two, match
Printing Offset
Software Adobe Photoshop,
QuarkXPress

Concept Wong, until recently an
employee for a major photo studio,
needed to establish his own identity
quickly. This letterhead system
accomplishes this with the use of
blocks of a distinctive gold-yellow
(the client's name means yellow in
Chinese) and a compelling photograph, which attract the eye but take
up little space. The use of his photo
as well as his name helps differentiate
him from his former employer, as
well as from competing photographers.
Cost-Saving Technique The package
was designed to be printed on a
smaller A B Dick press, rather than a
larger and more expensive press, to
keep printing costs low.
Cost $3,000   **Print Run** 2,000

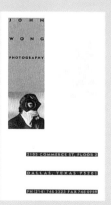

Art Director/Studio Steve
Keetle/Lundy.Keetle
Designer/Studio Steve
Keetle/Lundy.Keetle
Illustrator Lynd Ward
Client/Service Lundy.Keetle,
Burlington, VT/graphic design
Paper Neenah Environment, Desert
Storm
Type Memphis Extra Bold
Colors Two, match
Printing Offset
Software Aldus FreeHand

Concept As a new business design
agency, Lundy.Keetle used color to
make a strong impression. Dark,
environmental paper combines with
blocks of black and red and a 1930s-
style illustration of railroad workers
(to symbolize hard work) for visual
impact, while the oversized business
card further distinguishes the package. The large areas of red are meant
to give a feeling of revolution, sym-
bolizing the studio's emphasis on
creative thinking.
Cost $1,260 **Print Run** 1,000

Art Director/Studio Bryan L. Peterson/Peterson & Company

Designers/Studio Bryan L. Peterson, Dave Eliason/Peterson & Company

Client/Product Acme Rubber Stamp Co., Dallas, TX/rubber stamps

Paper French Dur-o-tone Butcher, off-white

Type Bell Gothic, Franklin Gothic, Trade Gothic

Colors Two, match

Printing Offset, rubber stamping

Software Adobe Illustrator, QuarkXPress

Concept The butcher-paper texture of this paper gives it an immediate presence—distinctive, but utilitarian. That sensibility, echoed in the generic industrial look of the letterhead, suits the client's name, business and location. Stamping the company name in red ink brightens the page and allows potential clients to see how the rubber stamps look.

Cost-Saving Techniques Hand-stamping gave this two-color job a three-color look. Design was free.

Cost $1,300   **Print Run** 2,000

EXPEDITIONS FOR YOUNG ADULTS
MIKE & HELEN COTTINGHAM
P.O. BOX 2768
JACKSON HOLE, WY 83001

MIKE & HELEN COTTINGHAM
DIRECTORS

EXPEDITIONS FOR YOUNG ADULTS
P.O. BOX 2768
JACKSON HOLE, WY 83001
307-733-2122
RECYCLED PAPER

EXPEDITIONS FOR YOUNG ADULTS
MIKE & HELEN COTTINGHAM
P.O. BOX 2768
JACKSON HOLE, WY 83001
307-733-2122

RECYCLED PAPER

Art Director/Studio Laura Quinlivan/
Riddell Advertising & Design
Designer/Studio Laura Quinlivan/
Riddell Advertising & Design
Illustrators Laura Quinlivan, Ruth
Harmon, found Native American art
Client/Service Wilderness Ventures,
Jackson Hole, WY/expeditions for
young adults
Paper Simpson EverGreen, Birch
Type Lithos
Colors Four, match
Printing Offset
Software QuarkXPress, Adobe
Photoshop

Concept Bright inks, a novelty typeface and Native American petro-
glyphs communicate the imaginative
nature of the client's business,
appealing to the parents who receive
the mail as well as to the children
who take the trips. The loosely struc-
tured style conveys the feeling of the
experiences participants encounter.
Cost $8,591   **Print Run** 35,000

TYPE

Designers of a certain bent find type fascinating, and will spend long hours modifying or designing typefaces and arranging words in classic or avant garde layouts that consist only of letters, numbers and dingbats. It's a rare client who shares that fascination. However, type-centered designs are well suited to letterhead.

A letterhead package may catch the reader's eye with its colors and graphics, and appeal to his or her fingers with its paper stock. But it's the type—the name, address and phone—that's crucial. That's the part that means business to your client.

Most letterhead designs require type that's easy to read, so classic roman and sans serif faces are ever-popular. But for the right client, difficult or unusual type—if it's arranged well—may make a better impression.

Before attempting a deconstructivist design for your next client's letterhead, ask yourself if the style makes sense for your client's business, and more importantly, if your client's clients will bother to read it.

If the answer to both questions is yes, follow the lead of several designers featured in this section. But if the answer is no, don't despair. As the featured packages that follow show, type-centered design that uses classic faces doesn't have to be boring.

Art Director/Studio Carolyn Lastick/ Carolyn Lastick Design

Designer/Studio Carolyn Lastick/ Carolyn Lastick Design

Client/Service Carolyn Lastick Design, Avondale, PA/jewelry design

Paper Japanese Facade, Cream by Vicki Schober Papers

Type Univers

Colors Two, match

Printing Offset

Software Adobe Photoshop, QuarkXPress

Concept A graphic designer with a jewelry design business on the side, the designer created a card that combined typeset letters with hand-drawn ornaments. The ink colors complement the exceptionally textured paper, while the ornaments reflect the style of Lastick's jewelry.

Cost-Saving Technique The designer bought her own paper and supplied it to the printer.

Cost $125

Print Run 500

Art Director/Studio Earl Gee/Earl Gee Design

Designer/Studio Earl Gee/Earl Gee Design

Client/Service Earl Gee Design, San Francisco, CA/graphic design

Paper Champion Kromekote

Type Univers 75

Colors Two, match

Printing Offset

Software QuarkXPress

Concept Originally designed for a speaking tour in the People's Republic of China, which required Chinese translations on the back of all business cards, this card reflects the Chinese American designer's heritage. Red and black make a bold statement, saturating the surface and contrasting starkly with the reversed-out type.

Type The letter *G* and the Chinese character on the reverse side both demonstrate how to pronounce the designer's name. The simple sans serif English type and complex, old-style Chinese characters work equally well in this design.

Cost $527.50

Print Run 1,000

Art Director/Studio Terry Laurenzio/ 246 Fifth Design Inc.

Designers/Studio Terry Laurenzio, Greg Tutty/246 Fifth Design

Client/Service Joy Parks, Gloucester, Ontario, Canada/writer

Paper Fox River Circa Select Concrete Recycled

Type Copperplate, hand-lettering

Colors Two, match

Printing Offset

Software QuarkXPress

Concept A description of the client's services in her own handwriting forms the background for this card, graphically portraying her profession and providing an unusual juxtaposition with the classic typeface. Ink only slightly darker than the textured paper makes the front blend with the back.

Special Visual Effect A screened rectangle, slightly larger than the client's name and address, makes the blue type readable.

Print Run 1,000

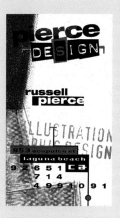

Art Director/Studio Russell Pierce/
Pierce Design
Designer/Studio Russell Pierce/
Pierce Design
Client/Service Pierce Design,
Laguna Beach, CA/graphic design
Paper Neenah Whitestone Classic
Laid
Type Dynamoe, Helvetica Extended,
Badloc Compressed
Colors Two, match, and one, process
Printing Offset
Software QuarkXPress, Painter X2,
Aldus FreeHand, Adobe Photoshop

Concept Produced solely on a computer, this package has a high-tech
look that nevertheless doesn't shout
"computer design." Punch label-style
lettering, layered type and graphics,
and intense colors give the piece a
post-industrial feel, yet skillful placement of these elements makes them
readable and functional.
Type The contrasting typefaces work
well together, commanding the extra
attention needed to read the address
and phone number.
Cost $750 **Print Run** 1,000 (letter-
head and cards), 2,500 (envelopes)

Art Director/Studio Richard L. Smith/
Steelhaus
Designer/Studio Richard L. Smith/
Steelhaus
Client/Service Steelhaus,
Chattanooga, TN/graphic design
Paper Neenah UV Ultra, Cross
Pointe Genesis, Simpson Quest
Type Stone Sans
Colors Two, match
Printing Offset
Software Aldus FreeHand

Concept Less is more for this piece,
which features tiny type, small graphics, and translucent paper. The design
makes maximum use of negative
space, creating a powerful impression
while leaving most of each piece
blank. Printing on both sides of the
vellum business card and letterhead
creates multiple layers and encour-
ages readers to handle the pieces.
Type Though tiny, the sans serif face
is attractive and easy to read.
Cost $0 (design traded for printing)
Print Run 500

BECKLEY IMPORTS INC.

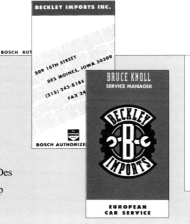

Art Director/Studio John Sayles/
Sayles Graphic Design
Designer John Sayles/Sayles
Graphic Design
Illustrator John Sayles
Client/Service Beckley Imports, Des
Moines, IA/automotive repair shop
Paper James River Graphika
Type Futura, hand-lettering
Colors Two, match
Printing Offset

Concept This package doesn't look
much like letterhead for a mechan-
ic—but the client wanted to differentiate his shop, which specializes in
repairing fine European automobiles,
from typical car repair shops. The
client's logo was inspired by
European car trademarks. Futura,
with its fat, friendly but efficient letters, completes the design. Bold
graphics and colors on bright white
paper demand attention, yet all pieces
were inexpensively produced by a
quick printer.
Print Run 1,500

Art Director/Studio Supon Phornirunlit/Supon Design Group
Designers/Studio Supon Phornirunlit, Dianne Cook/Supon Design Group
Client/Service Supon Design Group International Book Division, Washington, DC/book publishing
Paper Neenah Environment, Moonrock
Type Modula, Futura Condensed
Colors Two, match
Printing Offset
Software Adobe Illustrator, Aldus PageMaker

Concept For the book division of this well-known firm, the designers wanted to establish the image of an independent, progressive organization. The lighthearted three-color logo helps differentiate this group from the design studio, while the design style ties them together.
Type The main typeface, Futura Condensed, works well with the design. Its lean capitals create visual blocks and lines of copy without losing legibility.
Cost-Saving Technique The ink and paper stock are the same as those in Supon Design Group's main letterhead, so the two can be printed at once.
Cost $400 **Print Run** 500

SUPON DESIGN GROUP, INC.

INTERNATIONAL BOOK DIVISION

1000 CONNECTICUT AVE. NW

SUITE FOUR HUNDRED FIFTEEN

WASHINGTON, DC 20036

1000 CONNECTICUT AVE. NW

SUITE FOUR HUNDRED FIFTEEN

WASHINGTON, DC 20036

TEL: (202) 822-6540

FAX: (202) 822-6541

Supon Phornirunlit
Creative Director

SUPON DESIGN GROUP, INC.
INTERNATIONAL BOOK DIVISION
1000 CONNECTICUT AVE. NW
SUITE FOUR HUNDRED FIFTEEN
WASHINGTON, DC 20036
TEL: (202) 822-6540
FAX: (202) 822-6541

SUPON DESIGN GROUP, INC. INTERNATIONAL BOOK DIVISION

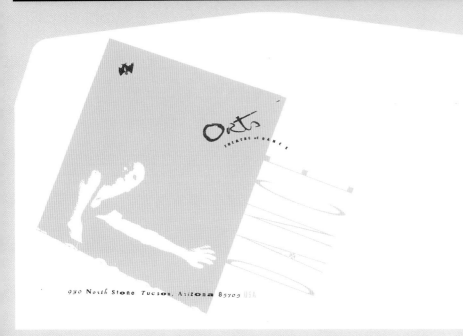

Art Directors/Studio Jackson Boelts, Eric Boelts/Boelts Bros. Design Inc.
Designers/Studio Jackson Boelts, Eric Boelts, Kerry Stratford/Boelts Bros. Design Inc.
Client/Service Orts Theater of Dance, Tucson, AZ/contemporary dance troupe
Type Various
Colors Two, match
Printing Offset
Software Aldus FreeHand, Aldus PageMaker

Concept Blocks of vibrant color, photostats of dancers, and a mix of typefaces and leading help give this package its dynamic look. Bright white paper adds contrast for further vibrancy. The client, a contemporary dance troupe, wanted to communicate its energy—especially to agencies giving grants to small arts groups.
Cost-Saving Technique Each piece was run in black plus one match color, for a four-color package at a two-color price.
Print Run 1,000

Art Director/Studio Jeremie White/
Suburbia Studios Ltd.

Creative Director/Studio Mary-Lynn
Bellamy-Willms/Suburbia Studios
Ltd.

Designer/Studio Jeremie White/
Suburbia Studios Ltd.

Illustrator Jeremie White

Client/Service Chek TV, Victoria,
British Columbia, Canada/television
station

Paper Neenah Classic Laid

Type Copperplate, Coronet, Senator

Colors Two, match

Software Aldus FreeHand,
QuarkXPress

Concept The client was marketing a
bold, young attitude and wanted a
progressive design that reflected the
name. The checkerboard logo,
echoed in the letterhead and envelope
design, plays on the name and provides a strong visual impact. Crisp
black bars provide a dramatic background for the two roman faces. The
second color, a light purple, is used
pointedly, creating a distinctive,
slightly cheeky attitude. The letterhead and fold-out business card both
use full-bleed art; to save money, the
envelope design uses none.

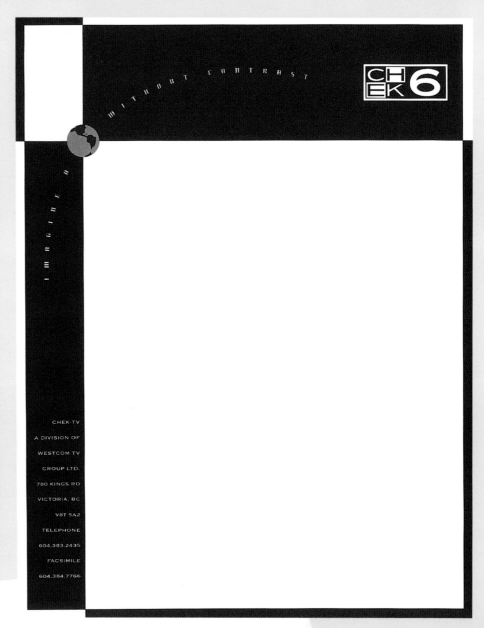

Art Director/Studio Michael Gericke/
Pentagram Design
Designer/Studio Michael Gericke/
Pentagram Design
Illustrator Eve Chwast
Client/Service Gwen Baker,
Livingston, NJ/public relations
consultant
Paper Strathmore Writing, Ivory
Type Stemple Garamond
Colors Two, match
Printing Offset
Software QuarkXPress

Concept Whimsical illustrations of
baked goods, playing on the client's
name, work with the classic type and
elegant cream paper for a timeless
design.
Type Crisp Garamond capitals and
illustrations with simple, heavy lines
together suggest letterpress, but at
much less the cost.
Cost $485 **Print Run** 1,000 (letter-
head and envelope), 500 (cards)

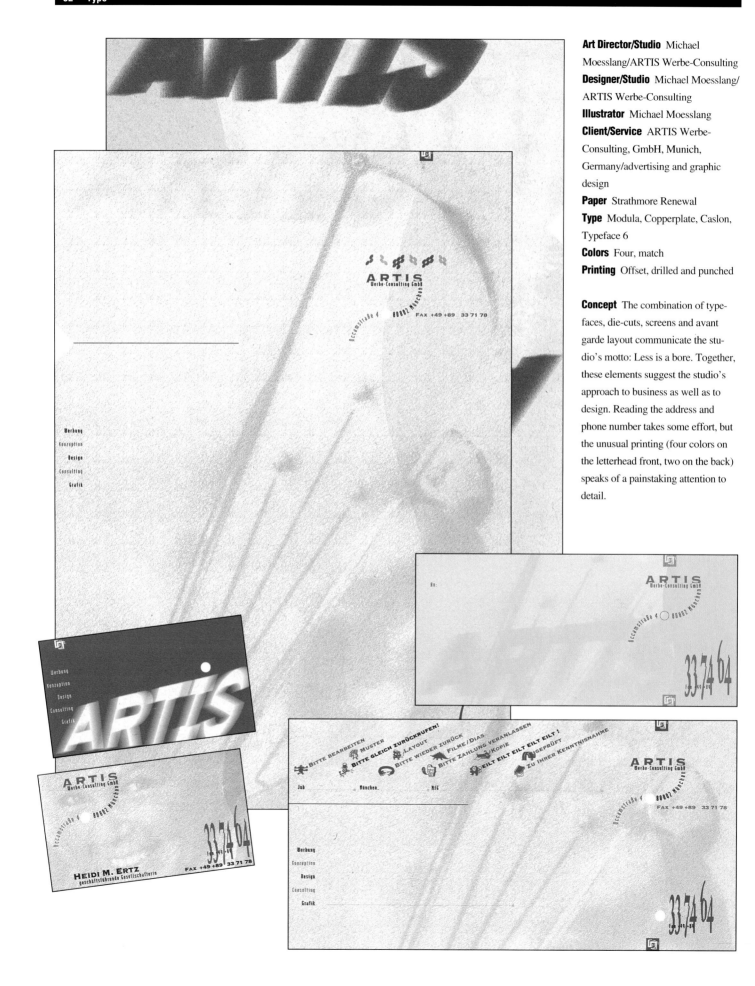

Art Director/Studio Michael Moesslang/ARTIS Werbe-Consulting
Designer/Studio Michael Moesslang/ARTIS Werbe-Consulting
Illustrator Michael Moesslang
Client/Service ARTIS Werbe-Consulting, GmbH, Munich, Germany/advertising and graphic design
Paper Strathmore Renewal
Type Modula, Copperplate, Caslon, Typeface 6
Colors Four, match
Printing Offset, drilled and punched

Concept The combination of type-faces, die-cuts, screens and avant garde layout communicate the studio's motto: Less is a bore. Together, these elements suggest the studio's approach to business as well as to design. Reading the address and phone number takes some effort, but the unusual printing (four colors on the letterhead front, two on the back) speaks of a painstaking attention to detail.

Art Director/Studio Vittorio Costarella/Modern Dog

Designer/Studio Vittorio Costarella/ Modern Dog

Illustrator Vittorio Costarella

Client/Service K2 Snowboards, Vashon Island, WA/snowboard manufacturer

Paper Simpson EverGreen, Birch

Type Futura Condensed

Colors Two, match

Printing Offset

Software QuarkXPress, Adobe Illustrator

Concept Unusual colors and a space age design give the client a consistent, professional look that also reflects the quirky nature of their business. The green bar containing the company name creates a memorable first impression.

Type The lean, bold character of Futura Condensed gives the letterhead an imposing presence, but the retro illustration and layout are a clue that this is tongue-in-cheek.

Cost $1,200 **Print Run** 1,500

Art Director/Studio Micheal Richards/Richards & Swensen
Designers/Studio Connie Christensen, Micheal Richards/Richards & Swensen
Illustrator Connie Christensen
Client/Service DareWare, Bountiful, UT/clothing design and manufacturing
Paper Strathmore Writing, Bright White, Wove
Type Syntax Ultracondensed
Colors Three, match
Printing Offset
Software Adobe Illustrator, QuarkXPress

Concept The curving address represents a T-shirt collar and the logo a hang-tag, working with the tiny clothing icons to suggest the client's business. The bright colors also suggest the client's young, fun approach to clothing design. The vibrant yellow bar catches a reader's attention, but leaves most of the page blank for easy faxing and photocopying.
Type Clothing pictograms function as dingbats, becoming part of an essentially all-type design solution.
Cost $2,000 **Print Run** 500

Art Director/Studio John White/ White Design

Designer/Studio Aram Youssefian/ White Design

Illustrator Aram Youssefian

Client/Service Pacific First Financial Securities, Long Beach, CA/broker

Paper Neenah Classic Crest, Solar White

Type Caslon Openface (company name), Garamond (address, title), Univers (employee name)

Colors One, match, and one, process

Printing Offset, engraving

Software Adobe Illustrator, QuarkXPress

Concept A timeless logo recalling currency communicates solidity and security, while the friendly but professional layout is meant to appeal to the client's audience: average investors.

Type A type-heavy design using traditional faces appeals to a conservative audience.

Print Run 5,000

Pacific Coast
Financial Securities

300 Oceangate, Suite 500, Long Beach, California 90802

Pacific Coast
Financial Securities

Pacific Coast
Financial Securities

Thomas A. Gans
President, General Securities Principal

300 Oceangate, Suite 500, Long Beach, California 90802
Tel. 310-983-6750, Toll Free 800-394-PCFS, Fax 310-983-6737

300 Oceangate, Suite 500, Long Beach, California 90802
Tel. 310-983-6750, Toll Free 800-394-PCFS, Fax 310-983-6737

Art Director/Studio John Sayles/
Sayles Graphic Design
Designer/Studio John Sayles/Sayles
Graphic Design
Illustrator John Sayles
Client/Service Advertising
Professionals of Des Moines, Des
Moines, IA/trade organization
Paper James River Graphika Vellum
Type Hiroshige, hand-lettering
Colors Two, match
Printing Offset

Concept The use of metallic ink and
a deep black envelope can't help but
catch a recipient's attention. This festive letterhead uses only type and a
special commemorative logo to
advertise a celebratory awards ban-
quet. Twenty-five stars, in honor of
the 25th anniversary, cover the letterhead and envelope without sacrific-
ing the legibility of any text.
Print Run 5,000

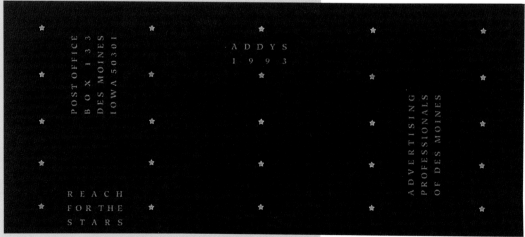

One
Fifth
Avenue

New
York,
NY
10003

ONE FIFTH AVENUE

Art Director/Studio Paula Scher/ Pentagram Design

Designers/Studio Paula Scher, Ron Louie/Pentagram Design

Client/Service One Fifth Avenue, New York City, NY/restaurant

Paper Mohawk Superfine

Type Bembo

Colors Three, match

Printing Offset

Software QuarkXPress

Concept Art, jazz and creative lighting formed the nucleus of Pentagram's redesign of this Manhattan restaurant. The letterhead system reflects the spirit of all three, at the same time playing visually with the restaurant's name and menu (One "Fish" Avenue). Light and airy, the design is pleasantly minimal.

Type Like lures, the restaurant name and address float, one word per line, before one-color photographs of fish.

Print Run 300

One
Fifth
Avenue

New
York,
NY
10003

(212)
529-1515

Art Director/Studio Andy Cruz/
Brand Design

Designers/Studio Andy Cruz, Rich
Roat/Brand Design

Client/Service Brand Design
Company Inc., Wilmington, DE/
graphic design

Paper French Dur-o-tone, Butcher
White (letterhead and business card);
cardboard (Stayflat envelope, address
file card); kraft (envelope)

Type Futura (name), Franklin Gothic
Condensed (deboss), Copperplate
(address)

Colors Three, match

Printing Letterpress (Stayflat envelope, Rolodex card), offset

Software Adobe Illustrator

Concept A combination of printing
techniques, papers and boards, and
inks give this type-based design
impressive variety and vitality. The
bold, industrial design makes a strong
impression, while metallic silver and
copper inks add an unexpected touch,
especially on the back of the business
card.

Cost-Saving Technique By letter-
pressing the cardboard pieces, the
designers could also afford to deboss
their name on the Stayflat envelope.

Cost $2,200 **Print Run** 2,000

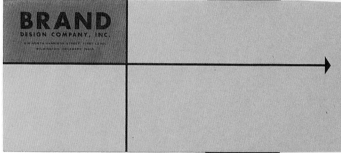

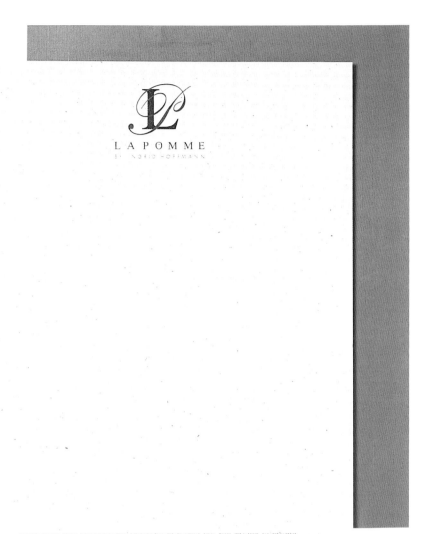

Art Director/Studio Maria Dominguez/Blue Sky Design
Client/Service La Pomme/ladies fashion boutique
Paper Neenah Classic Linen, Ivorystone
Type Times, Kuenstler Script Two Bold
Colors One plus varnish
Printing Offset, foil stamping, die cut
Software Aldus FreeHand, Aldus PageMaker

Concept Thick paper, metallic inks and varnish, and a simple, elegant design position this letterhead for a wealthy audience. The design also matches the store's decor, which features neoclassic architecture.
Special Printing Techniques This package's feel of luxury comes from printing techniques as well as from design. The store name and logo is foil stamped in two colors, while employee names are printed in gold metallic ink. The backs of the pieces are printed in a solid metallic gold, finished with a varnish. Business cards are die cut for their distinctive edge.
Cost $4,300 **Print Run** 1,000

Art Director/Studio Susan Hochbaum/Pentagram Design
Designer/Studio Susan Hochbaum/ Pentagram Design
Illustrator Rolla Herman
Client/Service Atomic Ironworks, New York City, NY/ironworks
Paper Gilbert
Type Bodoni
Colors One, match, and one, process
Printing Offset
Software Adobe Illustrator

Concept Pentagram designed the logo and catalog, as well as the letterhead, for this family-run ironworks. The cartoon-like logo reflects the spirit of the client's products: whimsical hat racks and candlesticks. The simple design solution suits the size and tenor of the client's business.

ATOMIC IRONWORKS 462 GREENWICH STREET NEW YORK, NEW YORK 10013 PHONE AND FAX 226.1510

Tom Nussbaum   Rolla Herman

Atomic Ironworks
462 Greenwich Street
New York, New York 10013
Phone and Fax 212 226.1510

SACKETT DESIGN   864 FOLSOM ST. SAN FRANCISCO, CALIFORNIA 94107   415.543.1590

SACKETT DESIGN   864 FOLSOM ST. SAN FRANCISCO, CALIFORNIA 94107

Art Director/Studio Mark Sackett/
Sackett Design Associates
Designer/Studio Mark Sackett/
Sackett Design Associates
Illustrator Chris Yaryan
Client/Service Sackett Design
Associates, San Francisco, CA/
graphic design
Paper Simpson Starwhite Vicksburg,
Tiara Smooth
Type Memphis (name), Times
(address)
Colors One, match, and one, process
Printing Offset
Software Adobe Illustrator

Concept Unusual colors and non-
standard sizes make readers give this
letterhead a second look. The square
paper folds in half, rather than in
thirds, to fit the standard-sized—but
vibrant green—envelope. Back-print-
ing the letterhead in two colors, with
the company name and logo, results
in each folded letter from the company resembling a mini-brochure pro-
moting the company.
Type An off-center type placement
gives a modern flair to the traditional
typefaces used in this package.

Art Director/Studio Michael Dunlavey/The Dunlavey Studio Inc.

Designer/Studio Heidi Tomlinson/ The Dunlavey Studio Inc.

Client/Service Earth Products Inc., Elk Grove, CA/landscape design and services

Paper Simpson Quest

Type 20th Century, Stuyvesant (name); Garamond 3 (address)

Colors Three, match

Printing Offset

Software Aldus PageMaker

Concept The illustration featured in this letterhead works well both in black and in full-color, and is also used on signs identifying client projects.

Type The unusual way script, serif and sans serif faces are combined on this letterhead complements the restful, organic quality of the artwork.

Cost-Saving Techniques Because the clients rely on their business card for new business, it is the only three-color piece. Letterhead and envelopes, rarely used, are quick-printed as needed.

Print Run 1,500

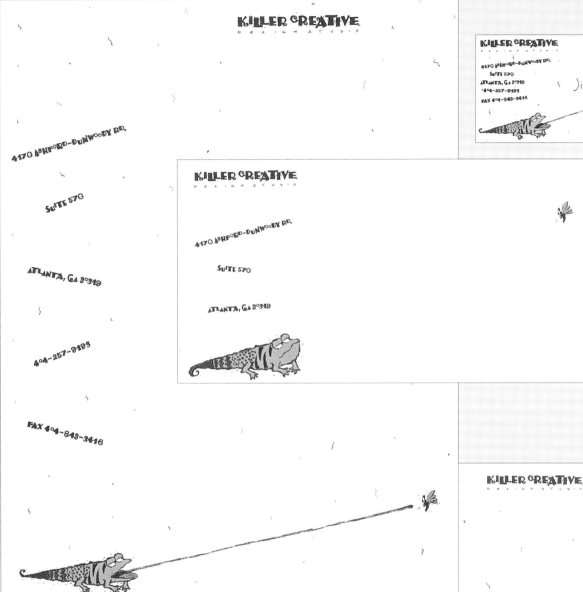

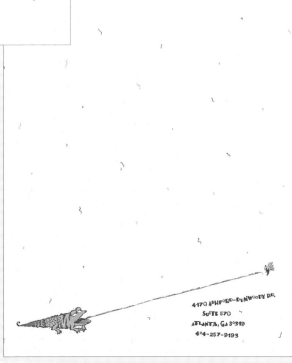

Art Director/Studio Beth Thomas/ Killer Creative Design Studio
Designers/Studio Beth Thomas, Gena Houghton/Killer Creative Design Studio
Illustrator Victor Kennedy
Client/Service Killer Creative Design Studio, Atlanta, GA/graphic design
Paper Strathmore
Type Sarah Elizabeth
Colors Three, match
Printing Offset

Concept Bright colors, an off-the-wall illustration, and unusual type come together to create this memorable letterhead. A colorful and casually-illustrated pattern creates a background that recalls both textured paper and confetti.
Type The hand-lettered look of this typeface adds to the cartoon-like quality of the entire package.
Print Run 2,500

Art Director/Studio Jack Anderson/ Hornall Anderson Design Works

Designers/Studio Jack Anderson, David Bates/Hornall Anderson Design Works

Client/Service CF2GS (Christiansen Fritsch Fiersdorf Grant and Sperry Inc.), Seattle, WA/marketing communications

Paper Curtis Brightwater, Artesian White

Type Copperplate, Futura, Caslon, Bodoni

Colors Four, match

Printing Offset

Software Aldus FreeHand

Concept This type-based design solution creates a corporate feel but emphasizes the creativity needed in a marketing firm. Sprinkling different sizes of the five logo symbols on a solid teal background on the back of the letterhead and business card gives the system a playful yet professional feel; the darkness of the background also helps emphasize the texture of the paper.

Type The typographic logo makes the company's name graspable, and the variety of fonts and colors used within this one logo suggests the array of skills to be found among the company's five principals. Each principal's business card has a different design on back—each emphasizing a different symbol.

Special Visual Effect The same pattern printed on the back of the letterhead is also printed on the interior of the envelopes for the system.

Print Run 3,000

Design Team/Studio David Collins,
Judy F. Kirpich, Grafik
Communications Ltd.
Client/Service Grafik
Communications Ltd., Alexandria,
VA/graphic design
Paper Brightwater, Artesian White
Type Bodoni 2 (address); custom
face based on Futura (name)
Colors Two, match
Printing Offset
Software Adobe Illustrator, Aldus
PageMaker

Concept The designers chose a
clean, uncluttered look for their stationery because their work is so
diverse that they feared to peg them-
selves by using a strong style. The
typefaces are classic and graphically
neutral, giving all design emphasis to
the logo. The subtle stripe inherent in
the paper adds texture, while the back
of the business card and the edge of
the envelope flap are printed in solid
red for an unexpected punch.

Grafik
Communications, Ltd.
1199 North Fairfax St.
Suite 700
Alexandria, VA 22314
703.683.4686
Fax 703.683.3740

Judy F. Kirpich
Vice President, Creative Director

Grafik Communications, Ltd.
1199 North Fairfax St.
Suite 700
Alexandria, VA 22314
703.683.4686
Fax 703.683.3740

G R A F I K

G R A F I K

Grafik
Communications, Ltd.
1199 North Fairfax St.
Suite 700
Alexandria, VA 22314

G R A F I K

Art Directors/Studio Jackson Boelts,
Eric Boelts/Boelts Brothers Design
Designers/Studio Jackson Boelts,
Eric Boelts, Kerry Stratford/Boelts
Brothers Design
Client/Service Boelts Brothers
Design/graphic design studio
Paper Crane's Crest
Type Baskerville
Colors Two, match
Printing Offset

Concept The designers wanted their
letterhead to reflect many aspects of
their corporate and design style,
including creativity, communication,
humor, and a positive business outlook. To convey a quality image, they
kept the design simple and uncluttered, using traditional typesetting
and two ink colors per piece. The
back of each piece is printed a solid
color, ornamented by the firm's
address and tiny "critters." These animal pictograms are the focus of firm
promotions including T-shirts and
cookbooks.
Cost-Saving Technique The designers traded design for printing.
Cost $300 **Print Run** 2,500 (letter-
head and envelopes), 500 (cards)

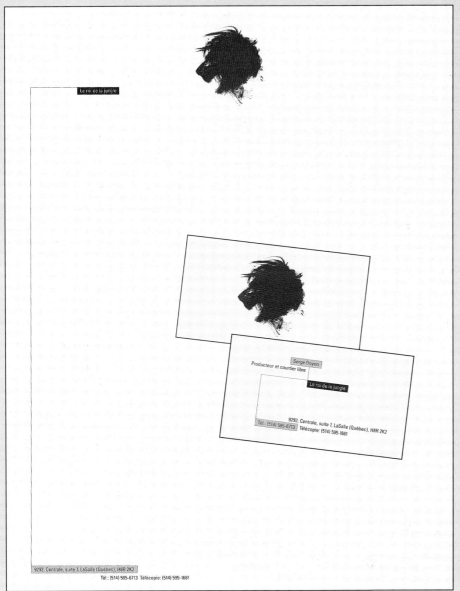

Art Director/Studio Steve Spazuk/
Tarzan Communication Graphique
Designer/Studio Daniel Fortin/
Tarzan Communication Graphique
Illustrator Steve Spazuk
Client/Service Serge Doyon,
LaSalle, Quebec, Canada/video
producer
Paper Rolland
Type Univers Condensed
Colors Two, match
Printing Offset
Software Adobe Photoshop, Adobe
Illustrator

Concept Seemingly random at first
glance, the swirl of brushstrokes at
the top of the letterhead depicts a
lion's head—the client's mascot.
Type The spare but readable face,
contained in colored bars for added
emphasis, effectively communicates
the client's address and phone number without distracting the reader
from the central image. This design
adapts well to the business card,
where the smaller area gives it added
presence. On the reverse side of the
card, the lion's head stands alone.
Print Run 2,000

VISUAL EFFECT

A well-designed letterhead gives the reader an instant, and accurate, impression of its owner. Whether the owner is a conservative financial advisor or a flamboyant restaurateur, the letterhead should reflect the client's personality and business, not the designer's.

When your client wants to make a powerful and unmistakable impression, you need to create a powerful and unmistakable design. You can pull out all the stops, using color, illustration, photography, and even unusually shaped paper to make sure your client gets noticed.

But powerful design doesn't always mean knockout colors and bold graphics. When used correctly, pale inks, conservative illustrations and classic typefaces can be just as effective—and for many clients, they're the only choice.

Whether wacky or staid, letterhead packages that make a strong visual statement are likely to provoke strong reactions. Recipients are apt to form instant and perhaps indelible perceptions of the sender. In other words, they're likely to either love or hate what they see. Clients willing to take the chance often find that though their letterhead may turn some potential clients away, it will also help them cement relationships with the audience they need most.

Art Directors/Studio Mark Friedman,
Mark Wasserman/Agency X
Designer/Studio Mark
Friedman/Agency X
Illustrator Warrent Sattunyue
Client/Service Tryst, Los Angeles,
CA/restaurant
Paper French Chipboard
Type Stempel Schneidler; 14th cen-
tury wood engraving
Colors Three, match, and two,
process
Software QuarkXPress

Concept The restaurant's neo-
European, romantic decor and evoca-
tive name inspired the old-world look
of this business card. The mysterious
imagery on the shield suggests hidden meanings and secrets, just as the
name suggests clandestine meetings.
Historic images and typefaces complete the picture.
Cost $1,000 plus $2,000 food trade
Print Run 2,000

Art Directors/Studio José Serrano,
Mike Brower/Mires Design Inc.
Designer/Studio Mike Brower/Mires
Design Inc.
Illustrator Miguel Perez
Client/Service John Piñza/personal
fitness trainer
Paper Strathmore Writing
Type Futura Book and Extra Bold;
custom face (name)
Printing Offset
Software Adobe Illustrator

Concept Because most of the client's
work comes from average but health-
conscious men and women of all
ages, the designers chose to portray a
fit, healthy figure rather than a body-
builder. The heavy white lines of the
illustration and type on the black
card exude strength.
On the other side,
the thin black type
on the crisp white
paper speaks of con-
fidence and profes-
sionalism. The client
also used this image
on t-shirts and sweat-
shirts.
Cost $3,500
Print Run 500

Art Director/Studio Michael
Dunlavey/The Dunlavey Studio Inc.
Designer/Studio Lindy
Dunlavey/The Dunlavey Studio Inc.
Illustrator Lindy Dunlavey
Client/Service River City Brewing
Co., Sacramento, CA/brew pub and
restaurant
Paper Champion Kromekote
Type Dolmen
Colors Three, match
Printing Offset
Software Adobe Illustrator

Concept The designers combined
type and illustration to create a hip,
urban image for a new microbrewery
in a renovated area of downtown
Sacramento. The figure of the running man gave the brewery an instant
personality, one that's contemporary
but based on industrial logos of the
1930s and 1940s. Because the logo
and address are also used extensively
on napkins, matches, bags, cups and
other collateral items, the designers
made sure that it would print well in
four-color process as well as with
match colors.
Print Run 2,500

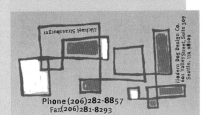

Art Director/Studio Robynne Raye/
Modern Dog
Designers/Studio Robynne Raye,
Michael Strassburger/Modern Dog
Illustrator Robynne Raye
Client/Service Modern Dog, Seattle,
WA/graphic design
Paper Simpson EverGreen
Type Meta (distorted)
Colors Two, process
Printing Offset
Software Adobe Photoshop,
QuarkXPress

Concept This is one design in a
series of letterhead packages intro-
ducing the off-the-wall design studio.
All use the same distinctive orange.
Reminiscent of 1950s-era art and cartoons, the letterhead leaves an indelible impression that is likely to cause
strong reactions from potential clients
and that leaves little doubt about the
firm's personality.
Cost $1,200 **Print Run** 1,500

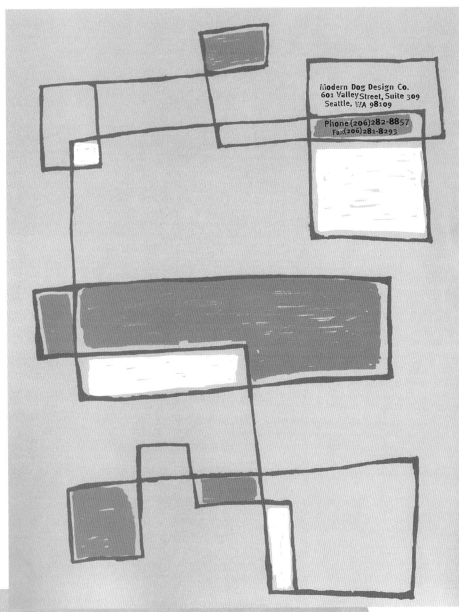

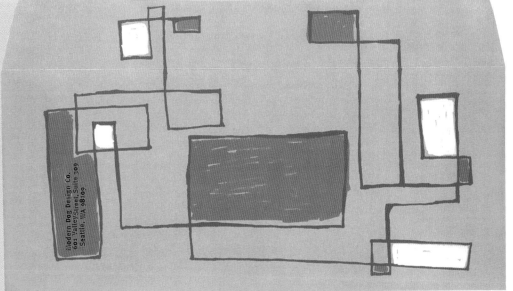

Art Director/Studio Lori Siebert/
Siebert Design
Designers/Studio Lori Siebert, David
Carroll/Siebert Design
Illustrator David Carroll
Client/Service Porter Printing,
Mt. Healthy, OH/printer
Paper Gilbert Writing
Type Bodoni
Colors Five, match
Printing Offset

Concept To reposition this printer
for an upscale market, the designers
chose bold colors and a design based
on printing that includes color bars
and register marks as graphics.
Metallic silver ink further contributes
to the upscale look, while fold-out
business cards add another intriguing
touch. The company eventually
adopted the design to vans, hats, jack-
ets and other collateral items.

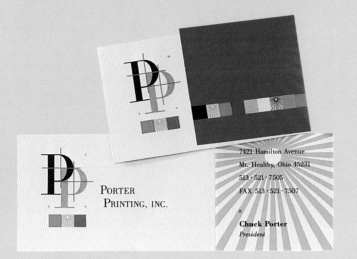

Art Directors/Studio Russ Willms, Jeremie White/Suburbia Studios Ltd.
Creative Director/Studio Mary-Lynn Bellamy-Willms/Suburbia Studios Ltd.
Designer/Studio Jeremie White/ Suburbia Studios Ltd.
Illustrator Jeremie White
Client/Service Suburbia Studios, Victoria, British Columbia, Canada/graphic design and illustration

Paper Neenah Classic Laid Recycled, Natural White (letterhead); Classic Duplex Recycled, Natural White and Peppered Bronze (card)
Type Insignia, Rechtman
Colors Two, match
Software Aldus FreeHand, QuarkXPress

Concept The studio chose to reflect the decor of its offices—suburban, warm, relaxed, and with a hint of Victorian style—in its two-color letterhead system. The slightly quirky system that resulted reflects what the designers call a sophisticated yet comfortable attitude, and demonstrates their design style without breaking their budget. Clean margins around all pieces but the business card create a frame for the design, and give the look of full-bleed art without its expense.
Cost $1,800 **Print Run** 5,000

Art Director/Studio Clifford
Stoltze/Clifford Stoltze Design
Designers/Studio Peter Farrell,
Clifford Stoltze/Stoltze Design
Client/Service Planet Interactive,
Boston, MA/multimedia presentation
developer
Paper Mohawk Poseidon
Type Meta, Officina
Colors Four, process
Printing Offset
Software Adobe Photoshop, Aldus
FreeHand

Concept Space-age graphics reflect
the company name, while four-color
printing represents the pixels of a
computer screen. The designers used
images of hands and curving lines to
convey the idea of interactive and
multi-media productions. Bright colors and a friendly layout help communicate that the company deals with
educational and corporate clients.
Print Run 5,000 (letterhead), 10,000
(second sheet), 15,000 (cards)

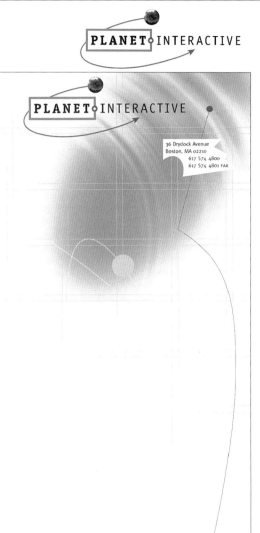

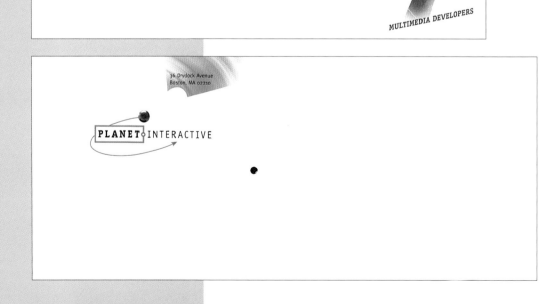

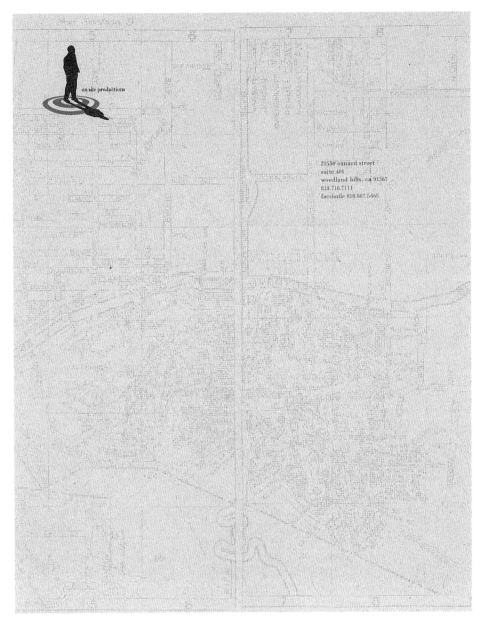

Art Director/Studio Brad Wilder/
Wordsmiths Advertising
Designer/Studio Brad
Wilder/Wordsmiths Advertising
Illustrator Brad Wilder
Client/Service on site productions,
Woodland Hills, CA/television and
film site location
Paper Simpson EverGreen Recycled
Type Bodoni
Colors Two, match
Printing Offset
Software Adobe Illustrator,
QuarkXPress, Adobe Photoshop

Concept The client wanted a different design solution from the expensive, glitzy letterheads that are the
entertainment industry norm. Dark
brown paper and simple two-color
graphics stand out strongly from the
foil-stamped, white-paper crowd. The
map and bullseye help communicate
the client's business, and the map
also shows the company's location.
Cost $1,800 **Print Run** 10,000 (let-
terhead and envelopes), 4,000 (cards)

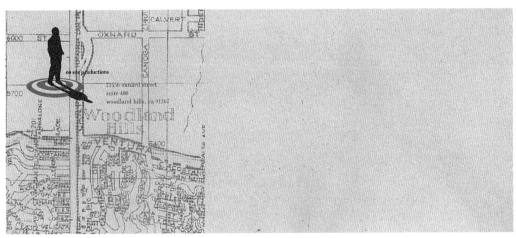

Designers/Studio Paige Keiser-Rezac, Steven Rezac/Fresh Squeezed Design

Client/Service Fresh Squeezed Design, a division of G.L. Ness Advertising and Marketing Inc., Fargo, ND/graphic design

Paper Ward Brite Hue Gold

Type Lithos

Colors Five, match

Printing Dry trapping

Software Aldus FreeHand, QuarkXPress

Concept To convey a youthful, freewheeling personality, the designers chose saturated colors and bold graphics. The bright gold paper conveys vibrancy and plays on the firm's unusual name.

Special Production Technique To produce saturated colors on the distinctive yellow paper, the printers first ran an opaque white, then dry trapped the purple and black, following them with the runs of opaque green and opaque red.

Cost $3,300 **Print Run** 1,000 (letterhead and envelopes), 3,000 (business cards), 600 (envelopes)

Art Director/Studio Laura Quinlivan/
Riddell Advertising & Design
Designer/Studio Laura Quinlivan/
Riddell Advertising & Design
Illustrator Jennifer Hewitson
Client/Service Aspen Travel,
Jackson Hole, WY/travel agency
Paper James River Graphika 100,
Spice
Type Akzidenz Grotesk Be
Colors Two, match
Printing Offset
Software QuarkXPress, Adobe
Photoshop

Concept Textured paper and elegant
graphics convey the client's upscale
business, booking travel for film production companies. The whimsical
logo, a buffalo jumping over the
moon, capitalizes on the firm's location and symbolizes its willingness to
go to any length to please its
clients—an important selling point in
a demanding business.
Cost $4,754 **Print Run** 2,000

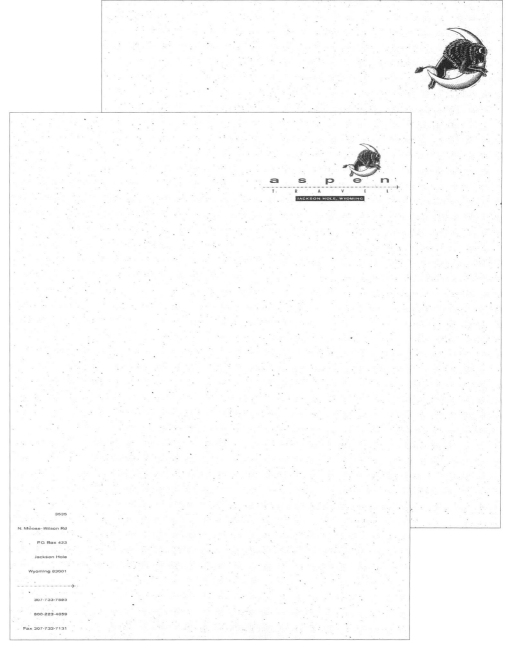

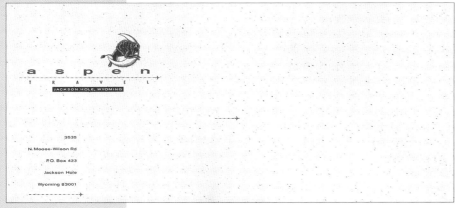

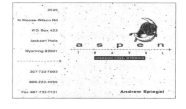

Art Director/Studio Mark
Sackett/Sackett Design Associates
Designer/Studio Mark
Sackett/Sackett Design Associates
Illustrator Wayne Sakamoto
Client/Service Donnelly &
Associates, Shawnee Mission,
KS/marketing and public relations
Paper Neenah Classic Crest, Natural
White
Type Copperplate
Colors Two, match
Printing Offset
Software Adobe Illustrator

Concept The designers used muted
green floral graphics to create a professional, neutral image for this
small, female-owned marketing company that had no particular area of
specialization. The design conveys
the feeling of a larger company,
because the marketer uses freelance
help to tackle large jobs. Cream paper
and a classic typeface further the
impression of competence.
Cost $5,100
Print Run Approximately 2,800

Art Director/Studio Peat Jariya/Peat Jariya Design

Designer/Studio Scott M. Head/ [Metal] Studio Inc.

Client/Service [Metal] Studio Inc., Houston, TX/graphic design products

Paper Champion Benefit, Neenah UV Ultra II

Type Matrix, Univers Condensed

Color One, black

Printing Offset, laser printing

Software Aldus PageMaker, Streamline, Adobe Illustrator

Concept The high-tech look of this system coordinates with the firm's existing print pieces. Unusual paper colors and printed backgrounds contribute to its slightly forbidding look. The letterhead is printed in-house and parts, such as labels, are laser-printed as needed.

Cost $3,700 **Print Run** 2,500

Art Director/Studio Martin Delves/
Niche Design Group
Designers/Studio Martin Delves,
David Pizzey/Niche Design Group
Client/Service Niche Design Group,
Fitzroy, Victoria, Australia/industrial,
graphic and engineering design and
consulting
Paper Saxton Smooth
Type Gil Sans
Colors Three, match
Printing Offset

Concept The eye-fooling logo communicates the firm's combination of
two- and three-dimensional work, as
well as the interdisciplinary nature of
many of its projects. Square sans serif
type and heavy orange bars convey a
technical, but aesthetically pleasing,
feel.
Cost $5,000 (Australian)
Print Run 2,000

NICHE
Second Floor
DESIGN
175 Brunswick St
GROUP
Fitzroy

Victoria 3065

Australia

Telephone

03 419 6835

Facsimile

03 416 4250

Art Director/Studio Terry Laurenzio/
Designers/Studio Terry Laurenzio,
Greg Tutty/246 Fifth Design
Client/Service Custom Printers of
Renfrew, Renfrew, Ontario,
Canada/printers
Paper Circa 83 Recycled, Hemp
Type Radiant Bold Condensed
(name), Univers (address)
Colors Five, match
Printing Offset
Software QuarkXPress

Concept The design of this letterhead system highlights the printer's
capabilities and thus, like most printers' stationery, also serves as a promotional tool. The five-color job displays the printer's skill with its
one-color presses, while the finely
detailed artwork shows its craftsman-
ship and attention to detail. The visuals also tie the historical aspects of
printing to its contemporary uses.
Print Run 3,000

Art Director/Studio Todd Hart/
Focus 2
Designer/Studio Todd Hart/Focus 2
Illustrator Todd Hart
Client/Service Mark Mahan
Photography, Dallas, TX/
photography
Paper Strathmore
Type Times Roman
Colors Three, match
Printing Offset
Software QuarkXPress

Concept The "say cheese" pictogram
reflects the photographer's personality and the fun, friendly style of his
work, while also communicating his
specialty—portraits. Simple typography and a neutral paper stock allow
the graphic to take center stage,
although the red background on the
business card ensures that the photographer's name and number can't be
overlooked.
Cost $2,500 **Print Run** 2,000

Mark Mahan Photography
3615 Gillespie, Suite H, Dallas, Texas 75219
214-521-8448

Mark Mahan Photography
3615 Gillespie, Suite H, Dallas, Texas 75219
214-521-8448

Mark Mahan Photography
1900 West 32nd Avenue Studio #5
Denver, Colorado 80211
303-455-8640

Art Director/Studio Terry Laurenzio/
246 Fifth Design Inc.
Designer/Studio Terry Laurenzio/
246 Fifth Design Inc.
Illustrator Terry Laurenzio
Client/Service 246 Fifth Design Inc.,
Ottawa, Ontario, Canada/graphic
design
Paper Mohawk Superfine, Eggshell
Type Lithos
Colors Four, process
Printing Offset
Software QuarkXPress

Concept A rich paisley design and a
distinctive typeface make this letterhead memorable, and highlights the
firm's style. The unusual letterhead
format draws further attention to the
design. Weighty paper stock and full-
bleed art on both sides of each piece
contributes to the package's impact.
Print Run 2,000

Art Director/Studio Susan Muldoon/
M Design
Designer/Studio Susan Muldoon/
M Design
Illustrator Susan Muldoon
Client/Service Tom Curran, Boston,
MA/videographer
Paper Loe Dull, Cover (rate and
business cards); Strathmore Bright
White Wove (letterhead and enve-
lope); Satin Crack 'n Peel (labels)
Type Bureau Agency
Colors Two, match
Software Sketcher, Aldus FreeHand

Concept The logo identifies the photographer's position as an independent cameraman, at the same time
identifying his camera package. The
bright yellow ink and bright white
papers help Curran stand out from his
competition, especially on the labels
he places on his tapes and equipment.
Cost $4,362 **Print Run** 1,000

Art Director/Studio Thomas Scott/ Eye Noise

Designer/Studio Thomas Scott/Eye Noise

Illustrator Clint Hansen

Client/Service Walt Disney World Resort Design, Walt Disney World, FL/resort properties

Paper Cross Pointe Genesis Script, Milkweed and Musk

Type ITC Century Bold and Expanded

Colors Three, match (letterhead), and two, match (envelope)

Printing Offset

Software Adobe Illustrator

Concept For stationery that doubles as a resort souvenir, the designer included Disney characters in Wild West attire. Rustic colors and type complement the border design and textured paper. The letterhead, smaller than business stationery, is printed on the reverse side in the rusty red of the type, as is the inside of the envelope.

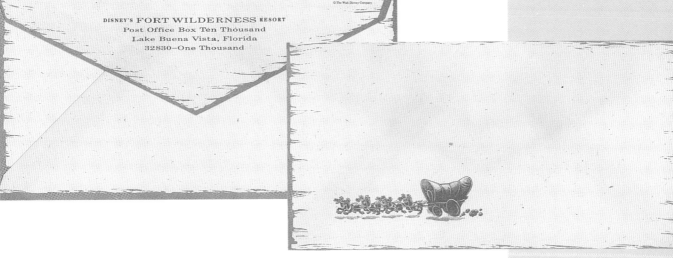

Art Director/Studio John Sayles/
Sayles Graphic Design
Designer/Studio John Sayles/Sayles
Graphic Design
Illustrator John Sayles
Client/Service I. A. Bedford, Des
Moines, IA/collegiate sportswear
manufacturer
Paper James River Graphika Vellum
Type Glypha, hand-lettering
Colors Five, match (three per piece)
Printing Offset, embossed and die cut

Concept Photocopies of fabric sam-
ples used for mechanicals convey the
client's sportswear manufacturing
business at a glance. The logo is reminiscent of many collegiate designs,
particularly sports team logos. The
unusual shape of the business cards
and letterhead echoes the logo, and
contributes to the system's overall
lighthearted quality.
Print Run 5,000

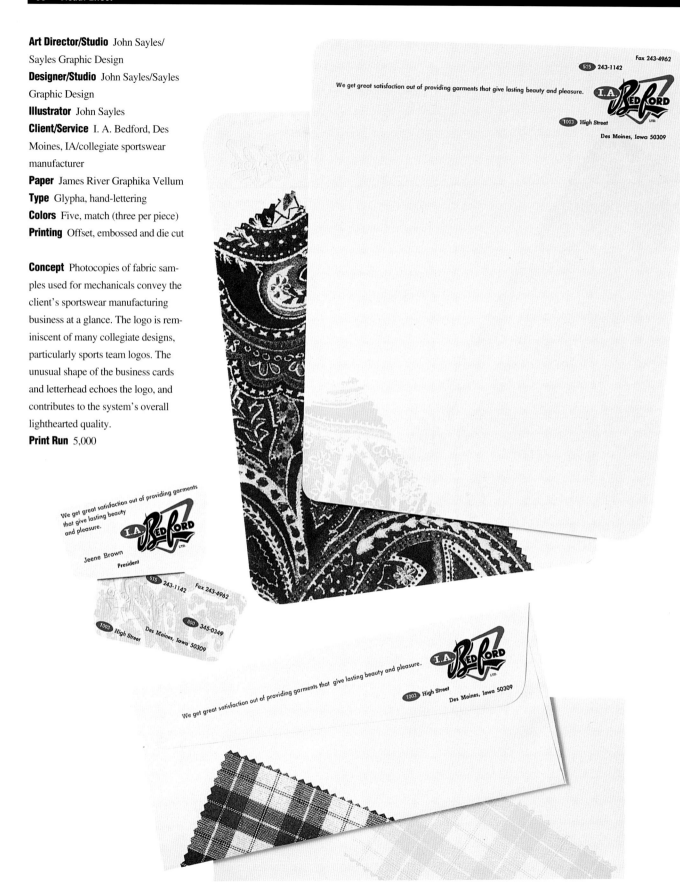

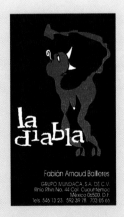

Art Director/Studio Ibo Angulo/
Zappata Diseñadores
Designers/Studio Ibo Angulo,
Claudio Anaya, Ana Maria
Lavalle/Zappata Diseñadores
Client/Service La Diabla, Mexico
City, Mexico/bar and nightclub
Paper White Holland Opaline
Type Avant Garde Condensed
(address), custom face (name)
Colors Two, match
Printing Screen printing
Software Aldus FreeHand

Concept La diabla—a mischievous
female devil—is depicted in a
Picasso-esque manner, the illustration
complementing the custom type to
communicate a definite personality.
The illustration also reflects the bar's
decor, which is based on Mexican
traditions. Screen printing gives this
piece its heavy, saturated colors.
Cost $5,000 (including collateral)
Print Run 2,000 (cards), 1,000
(letterhead and envelopes)

Art Director/Studio Toni Schowalter/
Schowalter 2 Design
Designer/Studio Toni Schowalter/
Schowalter 2 Design
Illustrator Toni Schowalter
Client/Service Commercial Design
Group, Summit, NJ/contract interior
design
Paper Curtis Flannel, Natural White
Type Helvetica Condensed
Colors Two, match
Printing Offset
Software QuarkXPress

Concept The architectural blueprint
engraving used for the letter *C* provides the client with a graphic typical
of decorative accents used in upscale
interior design. The system's elegant
simplicity suited the business and its
conservative clients. Textured paper
in a neutral, eggshell color and simple, straightforward type suggest the
interior designer's approach to her
work.
Cost $2,400 **Print Run** 1,000

Commercial Design Group

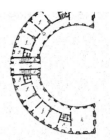

Lori Margolis

Commercial Design Group

43 Greenbriar Drive
Summit, NJ 07901
Tel 908.277.2880
Fax 908.277.0508

Interior Design
Space Planning

Commercial Design Group

43 Greenbriar Drive
Summit, NJ 07901

43 Greenbriar Drive
Summit, NJ 07901
Tel 908.277.2880
Fax 908.277.0508

Interior Design
Space Planning

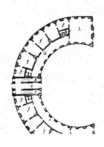

P.O. Box 255252 ■ SACRAMENTO, CA 95865

SACRAMENTO COUNTY FAIR

P.O. Box 255252

SACRAMENTO, CA 95865

(916) 263-2975

FAX (916)263-2973

A Presentation by the 52nd District Agricultural Association

100% Recycled Paper

Art Director/Studio Michael Dunlavey/The Dunlavey Studio Inc.
Designer/Studio Heidi Tomlinson/ The Dunlavey Studio Inc.
Illustrator Heidi Tomlinson
Client/Service 52nd District Agriculture Association, Sacramento, CA/Sacramento County Fair organizers
Paper Simpson Quest, Text
Type 20th Century, Linoscript, Dolmen
Colors Four, match
Printing Offset
Software Aldus PageMaker

Concept The designer's task was to create an identity for a fair that had none. The checkered clown, holding a "plate" of fun, fair-related items, personalizes the event. Bright colors and patterns contribute to the festive look. The clown and other items can also be pulled out and used as stand-alone icons for signs and other fair graphics.

Sacramento County Fair

CECILIA "CEESE" SMITH

P.O. Box 255252
SACRAMENTO, CA 95865
(916)263-2975
FAX (916)263-2973

A Presentation by the 52nd District Agricultural Association

Art Director/Studio Kelli Christman/ Free Range Chicken Ranch
Designers/Studio Kelli Christman, Tony Parmley/Free Range Chicken Ranch
Illustrator Kelli Christman
Client/Service Free Range Chicken Ranch, Campbell, CA/advertising and design
Paper Fox River Confetti (letterhead and card), kraft (envelopes), Neenah UV/Ultra II (postcard)
Type Matrix, hand-lettering

Colors Two, match
Printing Offset
Software Adobe Illustrator, QuarkXPress
Concept A combination of earth-tone-tinted papers and metallic ink introduces readers to the agency, which sees itself as both fun and down-to-earth. The custom no. 14 policy envelopes, left unprinted, help the agency's mail stand out but cost no more to send. Fold-out business cards also deliver greater impact.

Special Printing Techniques The metallic ink was printed twice to ensure that it showed up on a dark background. For the business cards, purple ink was specially matched to purple stock, so that it looks as if it were printed on both sides.
Cost $2,700
Print Run 2,500 (letterhead), 3,000 (cards), 3,425 (envelopes), 500 (post-cards)

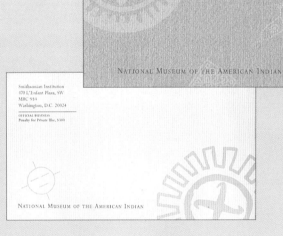

Design Team/Studio Julie Sebastianelli, Melanie Bass, Judy Kirpich/Grafik Communication Ltd.

Illustrator Linley Logan

Client/Service National Museum of the American Indian, Smithsonian Institute, Washington, DC/museum

Paper Gilbert ESSE Medium Gray/Green (letterhead and envelopes); Light Gray Red (business cards and notecards)

Type Lapidary, Gil Sans

Colors Five, match

Printing Offset

Software QuarkXPress, Aldus PageMaker

Concept To convey the museum's mission to portray a living culture, the designers used both traditional and contemporary Indian symbols representing the sun, earth and sky. The colors reflect those used in Indian pottery and weaving, and the paper has a handmade feel. The simple design represents Indian culture in a dignified, yet playful way, and allows room for many different staff names, addresses and titles.

Special Production Technique To ensure their opacity on the notecards and business cards, the symbols were run with one dry pass of opaque white underneath the beige.

Print Run 5,000

Designer/Studio Kathryn Frund/The Guild Group
Illustrator Kathryn Frund
Client/Service Carol F. Chamberlin, New Haven, CT/landscape architect
Paper Strathmore Writing, Bright White
Type Gil Sans Condensed
Colors Four, match
Printing Offset
Software QuarkXPress

Concept The client, who specializes in residential garden design and site planning, requested an approachable and energetic look. Impressionistic garden sketches, rendered in vibrant inks (one color per piece), communicate the client's business in an approachable way, leaving most of the paper blank for an open, uncluttered look. The bright white paper stock enhances the friendly feel.
Print Run 1,000

CAROL F. CHAMBERLIN
LANDSCAPE ARCHITECT
34 TRUMBULL STREET
NEW HAVEN CT 06511

CAROL F. CHAMBERLIN
LANDSCAPE ARCHITECT
34 TRUMBULL STREET
NEW HAVEN CT 06511
203 777 2636

CAROL F. CHAMBERLIN
LANDSCAPE ARCHITECT
34 TRUMBULL STREET
NEW HAVEN CT 06511
203 777 2636

LANDSCAPE ARCHITECTURE
GARDEN DESIGN
SITE PLANNING

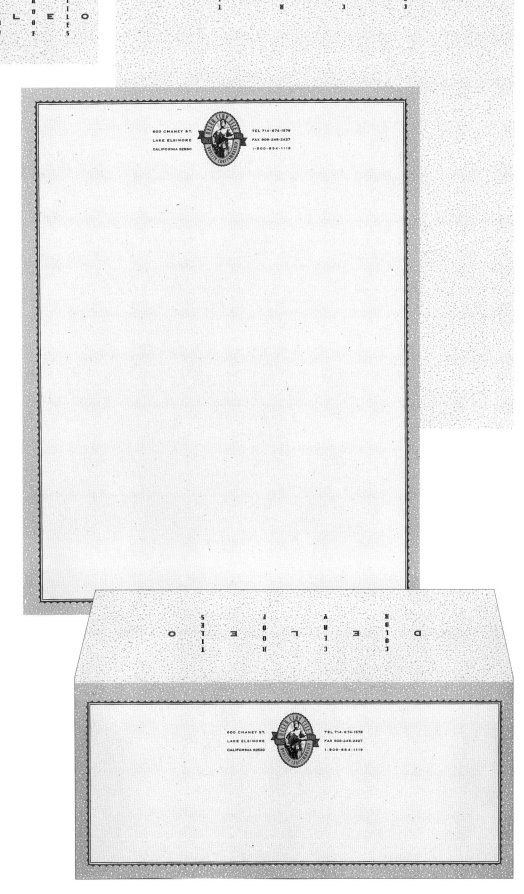

Art Director/Studio José Serrano/
Mires Design Inc.

Designer José Serrano/Mires Design
Inc.

Illustrator Nancy Stahl

Client/Service Deleo Clay Tile Co.,
Lake Elsinore, CA/clay roofing tile
manufacturer

Paper French Speckletone Kraft

Type Senator, Copperplate (address),
Matrix

Colors Three, match

Printing Offset

Software Adobe Illustrator

Concept The natural colors of the
papers and inks reflect the client's
business: manufacturing natural clay
roofing tiles. The decorative, clay-
colored border incorporates the shape
of the tiles, while the heroic figure in
the logo communicates the company's commitment to quality crafts-
manship in WPA style. Classic
Copperplate lettering further contributes to the trustworthy feel of this
design.

Print Run 2,000

Art Director/Studio Mark Sackett/
Sackett Design Associates
Designer/Studio Mark Sackett/
Sackett Design Associates
Illustrator Chris Yaryan
Client/Service AART Group,
Carmel, CA/art gallery
Paper Simpson Starwhite Vicksburg
Type Bodoni
Colors Two, match
Printing Offset
Software Adobe Illustrator

Concept To give a new art gallery
the impression of stability and experi-
ence, the designers incorporated classic design elements into a compre-
hensive letterhead system. Images in
a variety of styles represent the company's artistic breadth. The idea is
summed up in the company logo, a
composite frame. Smaller than usual,
the letterhead calls attention to itself
with its size as well as its design.
Cost $10,370 **Print Run** 5,000

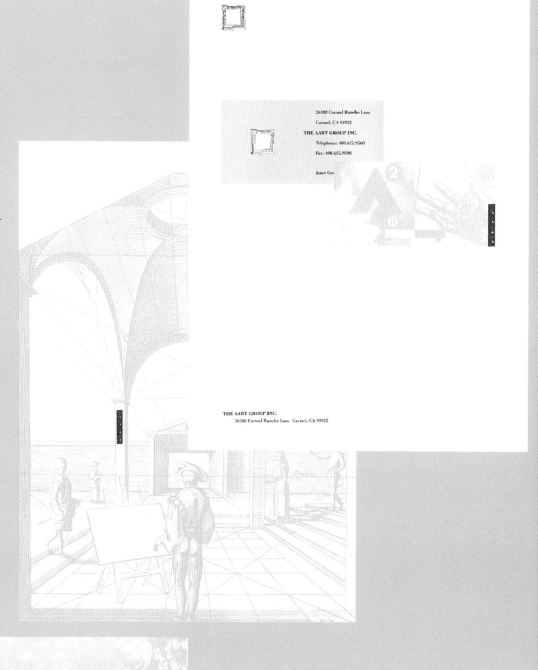

IMAGES**FRIEDMAN** GALLERY

833 West Main Street
Louisville, Kentucky 40202
502 584-7954

833 West Main Street
Louisville, KY 40202
502 584-7954

Art Director/Studio Julius Friedman/
Images
Designer/Studio Julius Friedman/
Images
Client/Service Images Friedman
Gallery, Louisville, KY/gallery
Paper Simpson Starwhite Vicksburg
Type Helvetica Black (name),
Stymie (address)
Colors Four, match
Printing Offset

Concept The kinetic feel of the circle, square and triangle create a memorable identity for an art gallery. The
composition and use of color reveal
at a glance the gallery's nature.
Cost-Saving Technique The designer
ran postcards, business cards, and
tags on one sheet of paper to save
printing costs.
Print Run 3,500

Art Director/Studio Alison Klassen/
Klassen Graphic Design
Designer/Studio Keith Petrus/
Klassen Graphic Design
Illustrator Keith Petrus
Client/Service Austin Natural
Science Association, Austin,
TX/nonprofit support group for the
Austin Nature Center
Paper Simpson EverGreen,
Cottonwood
Type Kabel
Colors Four, process
Printing Offset
Software Adobe Illustrator,
QuarkXPress

Concept This letterhead, which pro-
moted a special exhibit of animated
dinosaurs, had to appeal to patrons of
all ages. The illustration, which uses
existing photography, represents the
drama of seeing dinosaurs "come
alive." The type has a suitable prehis-
toric look, complementing the design
appropriately. The image, also
applied to posters, signs and T-shirts,
was popular with its target audience.
Cost $375 (billed); $1,625 (donated)
Print Run 3,000

DINOSAUR INVASION

The Austin Nature Center
301 Nature Center Drive
Austin, Texas 78746
512-327-2672

Sponsored by the Austin Natural Science Association

DINOSAUR INVASION

The Austin Nature Center
301 Nature Center Drive
Austin, Texas 78746

Non-Profit Organization
U.S. Postage Paid
Austin, Texas
Permit No. 2249

Art Director/Studio Michael Dunlavey/The Dunlavey Studio Inc.
Designer/Studio Lindy Dunlavey/The Dunlavey Studio Inc.
Illustrator Lindy Dunlavey
Client/Service World of Good Tastes, Sacramento, CA/restaurant chain operator
Paper Kimberly Writing, White Text
Type Xavier Sans
Colors Four, match
Printing Offset
Software Adobe Illustrator

Concept The vivid, kinetic illustration that forms the focal point of the package creates a new identity for an existing restaurant. Bright white paper stock shows the illustration to best advantage, while the unusual typeface continues its "wild" look. The firm also designed the restaurant's interior, inlaying the pictograms juggled by the central figure in the store's floor in brass.
Print Run 2,500

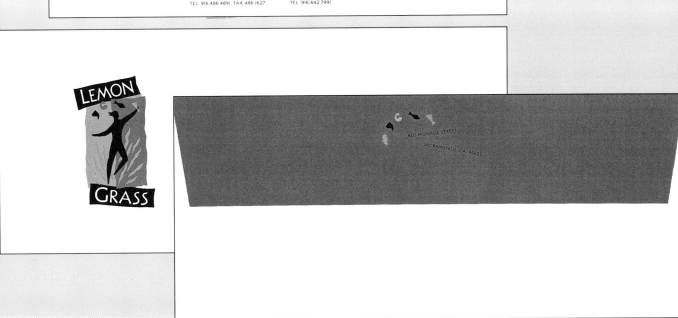

Art Director/Studio Michael Dunlavey/The Dunlavey Studio Inc.
Designer/Studio Heidi Tomlinson/ The Dunlavey Studio
Illustrator Heidi Tomlinson
Client/Service California Association of Winegrape Growers, Sacramento, CA/trade association
Paper Neenah Classic Crest, Natural White Writing
Type Sabon, Schniedler Initials
Colors Four, match
Printing Offset
Software Adobe Illustrator

Concept This new logo and letter-head design replaced a twenty-year-old system. The client, which lobbies for its members' interests, needed to convey an impression of solidity and service. The stylized grapes and grape leaf represent the association's agricultural base but are deliberately generic, so no one variety is depicted. Clean type and careful placing keep the letterhead from looking cluttered, despite the need to list many names and titles.

CALIFORNIA
ASSOCIATION OF
WINEGRAPE
GROWERS

OFFICERS
Brian Gebhart
  Chairman
Kevin Andrew
  Vice Chairman
John Kautz
  Vice Chairman
Kenneth Deaver
  Vice Chairman
Fred Lagomarsino
  Secretary
Kurt Gollnick
  Treasurer
Robert P. Hartzell
  President
Shirley A. Winston
  Vice President

BOARD OF DIRECTORS
District #1
Tom Ashurst, *Hopland*
Volker Eisele, *St. Helena*
Patrick J. Garvey, *Napa*
Brian Gebhart, *Santa Rosa*
Keith Kunde, *Glen Ellen*
Jim Ledbetter, *Healdsburg*

District #2
Kurt Gollnick, *King City*
Dale Hampton, *Santa Maria*
Paul Hope, *Paso Robles*
Richard R. Smith, *Soledad*
Edwin N. Woods, *Santa Maria*

District #3
John Kautz, *Lodi*
Randall Lange, *Acampo*
Richard Samra, *Clarksburg*

District #4
Bill Berryhill, *Ceres*
Kenneth Deaver, *Plymouth*
Ronald McManis, *Ripon*

District #5
Ray Jacobsen, *Fresno*
Fred Lagomarsino, *Tulare*
Eric Shannon, *Visalia*
John W. Simpson, *Madera*

District #6
Kevin Andrew, *Bakersfield*
Bridget Hildebrand, *Bakersfield*
John Wood, *Arvin*

District #7
Bennett R. Drake, *Temecula*

DIRECTORS-AT-LARGE
Barry Bedwell
Michael Hat
J. Gordon Lent
Hugh Macklin

225 30TH STREET, SUITE 306 ✦ SACRAMENTO, CA 95816 ✦ 916 448-2676 ✦ FAX 916 448-0475
Representing the Wine and Food Industry

ROBERT P. HARTZELL
President

Representing the
Wine and Food Industry

225 30TH STREET, SUITE 306
SACRAMENTO, CA 95816
916 448-2676 FAX 916 448-0475
HOME 209 569-4184

CALIFORNIA
ASSOCIATION OF
WINEGRAPE
GROWERS

225 30TH STREET ✦ SUITE 306 ✦ SACRAMENTO, CA 95816
Representing the Wine and Food Industry

CALIFORNIA
ASSOCIATION OF
WINEGRAPE
GROWERS

Bixler
Picture
Shows

2042 W. Fletcher
Chicago, IL 60618

Bixler
Picture
Shows

2042 W. Fletcher
Chicago, IL 60618

Art Director/Studio Judith Paolini/
Thibault Paolini Design Associates
Designer/Studio Judith Paolini/
Thibault Paolini Design Associates
Illustrator Barbara Emmons
Client/Service Bixler Picture Shows,
Chicago, IL/film producer and director
Paper Neenah Environment,
Woodstock (letterhead, envelope);
Mactac Starliner, Kraft (label)
Type Industria Solid
Colors Two, match
Printing Offset
Software Aldus FreeHand

Concept Energetic colors, type and
illustrations give this package a personality suited to the client, known
for her animated directing style. The
two-sided card identifies both the
client's main business and a second
production company. The piece was
also designed for a future addition: a
flipbook business card using the illustrations featured on the letterhead.
Cost $1,650 **Print Run** 500

Bixler
Picture
Shows

2042 W. Fletcher
Chicago, IL 60618
312 248 5430
312 248 5480 FAX

Kelli Bixler
Director

Bixler
Picture
Shows

presents

Snack Stix Productions, Inc.

Chicago

2042 W. Fletcher   60618   312 248-5430   312 248-5480 FAX

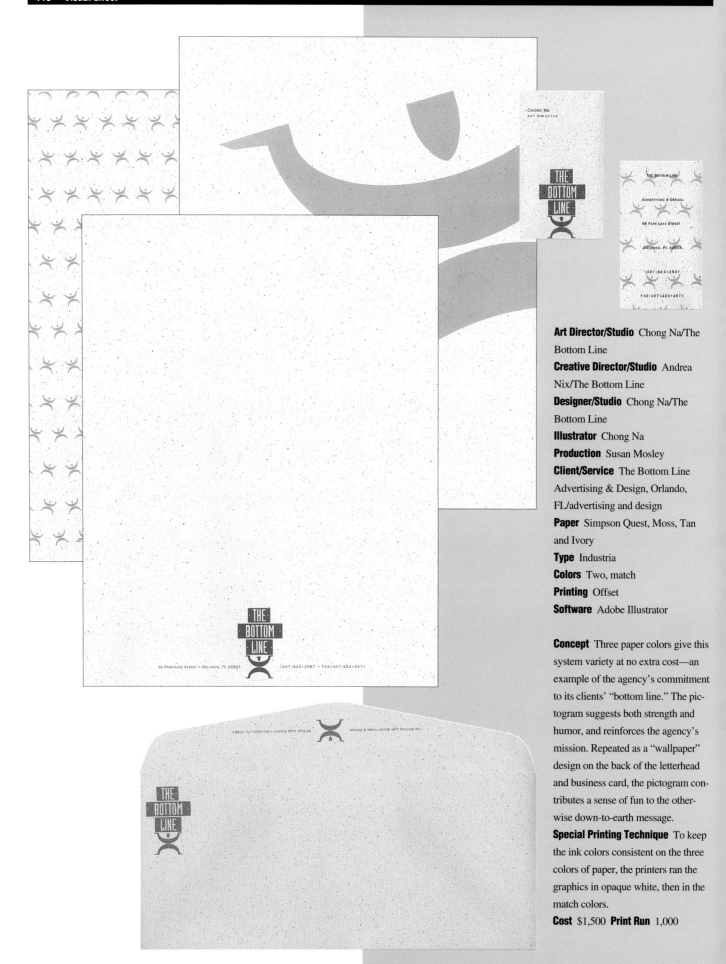

Art Director/Studio Chong Na/The Bottom Line
Creative Director/Studio Andrea Nix/The Bottom Line
Designer/Studio Chong Na/The Bottom Line
Illustrator Chong Na
Production Susan Mosley
Client/Service The Bottom Line Advertising & Design, Orlando, FL/advertising and design
Paper Simpson Quest, Moss, Tan and Ivory
Type Industria
Colors Two, match
Printing Offset
Software Adobe Illustrator

Concept Three paper colors give this system variety at no extra cost—an example of the agency's commitment to its clients' "bottom line." The pictogram suggests both strength and humor, and reinforces the agency's mission. Repeated as a "wallpaper" design on the back of the letterhead and business card, the pictogram contributes a sense of fun to the otherwise down-to-earth message.
Special Printing Technique To keep the ink colors consistent on the three colors of paper, the printers ran the graphics in opaque white, then in the match colors.
Cost $1,500 **Print Run** 1,000

Art Director/Studio Mark Sackett/ Sackett Design Associates
Designers/Studio Mark Sackett, Wayne Sakamoto/Sackett Design Associates
Illustrator Kim Howard
Client/Service Kim Howard, Ketchum, ID/illustrator
Paper French Speckletone, Madero White
Type Bodoni
Color One, black
Printing Offset
Software Adobe Illustrator

Concept To allow the client, an illustrator, to display her work, the designers created a simple grid of black type on textured paper. The illustrator then customizes every piece herself, adding whatever ornaments she desires. Although this requires considerable effort from the client, the package was inexpensive and it creates a constantly changing identity for her business.

SPECIAL PRODUCTION TECHNIQUES

They're often, but not always, expensive. And they're often, but not always, flashy. Whatever their look or price, special production techniques can make an indelible impression on your client's clients. There are so many to choose from that there's sure to be one technique to fit your client's image and budget. A folded business card, artwork or type applied with a rubber stamp, metallic inks, die cuts, varnishes . . . the list is nearly endless. For those with deep pockets, specialty business cards are particularly popular. But even these can be inexpensive, if you or your client is willing to put in some hours with scissors, staples and glue. As the systems in this section illustrate, even one special touch can give your clients the edge over their competition.

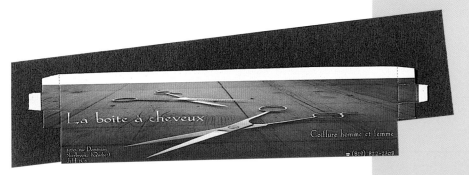

Art Directors/Studio Daniel Forin,
Steve Spazuk/Tarzan
Communication Graphique
Client/Service Brigitte Beaudoin,
Sherbrooke, Quebec, Canada/hair-
dresser
Paper Rolland Opaque Nouvelle Vie
Type Lilith Light
Colors Two, match
Printing Offset
Software Adobe Photoshop,
QuarkXPress

Concept This unusual card folds into
a long, thin box the size of a pencil.
Indeed, the client can enclose pens,
pencils, notes or other promotions in
it. A hairdresser (hence the photograph of trimming scissors), she often
uses the cards to hold locks of her
clients' hair, which she gives them as
souvenirs.
Print Run 3,000

Art Director/Studio William Kochi/
KODE Associates
Designer/Studio William Kochi/
KODE Associates
Client/Service Kode Associates,
Inc./graphic design
Paper Gilbert ESSE
Type Adobe Garamond (address),
Futura (name)
Colors Four, process
Printing Offset
Software Adobe Photoshop, Adobe
Illustrator

Concept This intriguing card
calls attention to itself both
folded and unfolded. Folded
into a two-inch square, it
forms a neat packet marked
only by the firm's name.
Unfolded into an *S* shape, it
reveals the other essential
information on one side,
remaining a colorful enigma
on the other.
Cost-Saving Technique Though the
cards were die cut and scored by the
printer, the designer folded them himself.
Cost $1,700 **Print Run** 2,000

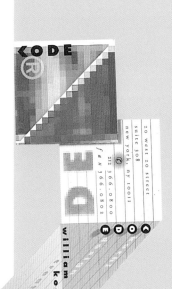

Art Director/Studio Alison Klassen/
Klassen Graphic Design
Designers/Studio Pete Herzog, Keith
Petrus/Klassen Graphic Design
Client/Service The Jollymen/handy-
men
Type Helvetica
Printing Rubber stamping
Software Adobe Illustrator,
QuarkXPress

Concept This short-run novelty card
is perhaps one of the most useful ever
designed: Clients can measure with
the accurate ruler that forms the top
border. Printed on birch wood with a
self-inking rubber stamp, this keepsake card uniquely communicates the
Jollymen's business.
Cost $690 **Print Run** 100

Art Director/Studio Thomas Hemann/Fish & Co.
Designer/Studio Thomas Hemann/ Fish & Co.
Client/Service David Castro/hair stylist
Type Various
Colors Four, process

Art Director/Studio Terri O'Hare/ O'Hare Design
Designer/Studio Terri O'Hare/ O'Hare Design
Client/Service Rod Mickley, Vero Beach, FL/interior design and accessories
Paper Neenah Environment, Woodstock, Creme (cover); U/V Sheet (interior)
Type Copperplate Bold
Colors Two, match
Printing Offset
Software QuarkXPress

Concept The client wanted to introduce his interior design style to potential clients, particularly at showcase homes, where he might not be present when they picked up the cards. The booklet card, designed to appeal to design-conscious people, includes two screened photographs of room interiors. The photos give an impression of Mickley's rooms, but the limited detail in the depiction ensures recipients won't be distracted by the particulars of the two rooms.
Cost $2,500   **Print Run** 1,000

Art Director/Studio Bonnie Phippen/ Phippen Design Group
Designers/Studio Sheldon Lewis, Bonnie Phippen/Phippen Design Group
Photographer Bonnie Phippen
Client/Service B&G Painting/commercial painting contractor
Paper Simpson Starwhite Vicksburg Tiara Cover Vellum
Type Edition Sans (name); Garamond (address)
Colors Two, match
Printing Offset, foil stamped

Concept The foil-stamped logo and architectural photography helped reposition this painting contractor as a more upscale business aimed at clients concerned with art and design. Because there was no photography budget, the designers negotiated with the client to choose four local buildings and pay for an hour of their time to shoot them. Because the photographs would be shot in natural light and ghosted on the card, the designers knew they could handle the job. The client also provided transportation for the shoot.
Cost $1,175   **Print Run** 1,000

Printing Offset
Software Aldus FreeHand

Concept Because the client relied on cards for marketing, he wanted something memorable to suggest that he could make clients look good. The fold-out design and random type logo communicate the hair stylist's creativity, while the twining curls of type inside suggest that he's fun to be around.
Cost-Saving Techniques The card was done on the same sheet as a four-

Art Director/Studio Jack Anderson/
Hornall Anderson Design Works
Designers/Studio Jack Anderson,
Heidi Hatlestad, Mary Chin
Hutchison, Bruce Branson-
Meyer/Hornall Anderson Design
Works
Illustrator Scott McDougall
Client/Service Print Northwest/Six
Sigma, Tacoma, WA/offset printing
and disk replication
Paper Neenah Classic Crest
Recycled
Type Futura Condensed
Colors Nine, match
Printing Offset
Software Aldus FreeHand, Adobe
Photoshop

Concept To integrate a 92-year-old
printing company with its new disk
replication division, the designers
created a new letterhead system using
both names. Produced with four different color schemes, the new package continued the printer's reputation
for innovative use of color. All papers
and inks are laser-compatible,
because of the rich colors printed on
the back of the letterhead. The deep,
even colors and the "halo" designed
into the logo demonstrate the printer's skill.

C h a l i f o u r

C h a l i f o u r

BENOÎT CHALIFOUR PHOTOGRAPHE 4297 REDWOOD, PIERREFONDS, QUÉBEC H9H 2C5 CANADA TÉLÉPHONE: (514) 620-6487

C h a l i f o u r

BENOÎT CHALIFOUR PHOTOGRAPHE
4297 REDWOOD, PIERREFONDS,
QUÉBEC H9H 2C5 CANADA
TÉLÉPHONE: (514) 620-6487
FAX: (514) 620-0259

Art Director/Studio George Fok/
Tarzan Communication Graphique
Designer/Studio George Fok/Tarzan
Communication Graphique
Illustrator George Fok
Client/Service Benoît Chalifour,
Pierrefonds, Quebec, Canada/photog-
rapher
Paper Gilbert
Type Bodoni
Colors Two, match
Printing Offset
Software Adobe Photoshop, Adobe
Illustrator

Concept An eye in a floating globe
makes a memorable symbol for this
on-location photographer.
Transparent cards and letterhead
reinforce the image of a cloudy sky
and the feeling of weightlessness.
The sky is also printed on the back of
more practical white stationery,
leaving only the globe symbol and
the photographer's name and address
to accompany the text.
Print Run 2,000

Art Director/Studio Steve Keetle/
Lundy.Keetle

Designers/Studio Steve Keetle,
Maureen Wulfson/Lundy.Keetle

Illustrator Steve Keetle

Client/Service Eye of the Storm,
Burlington, VT/product development
and design

Paper Strathmore Writing, Ultimate
White

Type Caslon 540

Colors Four, match

Printing Offset

Software QuarkXPress

Concept The client wanted to convey its energy and creativity in a con-
ceptual, non-traditional way as origi-
nal as their name. Instead of a more
traditional logo, the designers created
one more like a piece of fine art. It's
as effective covering the entire surface of the back of the letterhead as it
is reduced on the corner of a Rolodex
card. The contemporary color
scheme, distinctive sizes, and unusual
angles of each piece communicate
the client's commitment to finding
aggressive and creative solutions.

Cost $3,535 **Print Run** 1,000

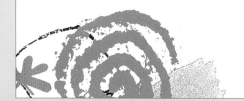

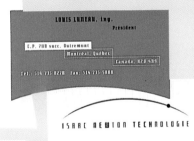

Art Director/Studio Steve Spazuk/
Tarzan Communication Graphique
Designer/Studio George Fok/Tarzan
Communication Graphique
Client/Service Isaac Newton
Technologie, Montreal, Quebec,
Canada/inventors
Paper Domtar MagnoDull
Type Senator (address), hand-letter-
ing (name)
Colors Four, match
Printing Offset
Software Adobe Illustrator

Concept Metallic inks and a distinctive curved edge echoing the company logo make this system stand out.
The clients, who specialize in high-
tech inventions, wanted a serious, but
inventive, futuristic look. Jagged type
and appropriate graphics create the
impression of a forward-thinking
company, while the die-cut paper and
cards invite readers to handle the
pieces and give them a second look.
Print Run 2,000

Art Director/Studio Terri O'Hare/
O'Hare Design
Designer/Studio Terri O'Hare/
O'Hare Design
Client/Service Krieghoff Guns, Vero
Beach, FL/imported collectible gun
sales
Paper Neenah Classic Crest Writing,
Wove, Avon Brilliant White
Type Futura Medium
Color One, match
Printing Offset
Software QuarkXPress

Concept Money was no object for
this client, who needed memorable
letterhead for use at trade shows, and
who wanted communications materials that were as unique as their product and that would appeal to discrimi-
nating buyers. Though the system
uses only one color, its die-cut holes
make a powerful design statement.
Together, the pieces suggest to recipients the quality of the guns, and the
staff who sells them.
Cost $4,700 **Print Run** 2,500

KRIEGHOFF
P.O. BOX 3528, BEACH STATION, VERO BEACH, FLORIDA 32964-3528
1-800-73-K-GUNS · 407-231-1221 · 407-231-6503 FAX

Art Director/Studio Walter N. Strump/Image Factory

Designer/Studio Walter N. Strump/ Image Factory

Photographer Donna Victor

Client/Service Image Factory, Miami, FL/advertising and graphic design

Paper Beckett Enhance, Ultra White (letterhead and cards); Gilclear, White (envelopes)

Type Futura Condensed (address), Madrid (name)

Colors Four, process, and one, match

Printing Offset

Software QuarkXPress, Aldus FreeHand

Concept Two-sided printing in exact registration is the key to this vibrant system. The photograph of cogs and gears represents the image "factory," a factory that produces more than one product. The text side of the letter-head features a ghosted version of this image, which is repeated full-strength on the back, as if the paper were translucent. The back of the let-terhead showing through the translu-cent envelope creates the same effect.

Cost-Saving Technique To save on future printing, the firm ordered many blank, untrimmed business cards that can be printed with new employees' names when needed.

Print Run 5,000

Art Directors/Studio Jesse Doquilo,
Randy Lim, Glenn Mitsui/Studio MD
Designers/Studio Jesse Doquilo,
Randy Lim/Studio MD
Illustrator Jesse Doquilo
Client/Service Studio MD, Seattle,
WA/graphic design and digital illus-
tration
Paper Strathmore Renewal Spackle
Writing and Text
Type Bank Gothic Light and
Medium, Helvetica Black
Colors Two,
match
Printing Offset
Software Adobe
Photoshop, Aldus
FreeHand

Concept To create what they refer to
as the "wow" factor, Studio MD
invested in die-cut, dimensional business cards. At thirty cents each the
cards are still a bargain, the designers
say, because clients keep them. And
although the cards fold to standard
size, Studio MD reports that their
clients tend to keep them out on their
desks rather than in their wallets or
files.
Cost-Saving Techniques The cards
are constructed of two pieces, one die
cut and one a simple box printed with
all the names of all four staff designers. The cards are custom-assembled
for each staffer.
Print Run 5,000 (letterhead); 7,500
(cards)

O & J

Design, Inc.

9 West 29th Street
New York, NY 10001

O & J

Design, Inc.

9 West 29th Street
New York, NY 10001
♪ 212.779.9654
◻ 212.779.9727

Andrzej J. Olejniczak

O & J

Design, Inc.

Art Director/Studio Andrzej
Olejniczak/O&J Design Inc.
Designer/Studio Inhi Clara Kim/
O&J Design Inc.
Client/Service O&J Design Inc.,
New York, NY/graphic design
Paper Crane's Crest
Type Frutiger
Colors Three, match
Printing Engraving
Software Adobe Illustrator,
QuarkXPress

Concept This system, a redesign of
an existing system, presents a crisp,
clean look that conveys competence
and clarity. The engraving literally
adds a second dimension. The raised
graphics on the stiff white paper
appeal to the fingers, and also implies
that the designers' work is of particularly high quality. Engraving generally suggests quality and stability. In
this context, it also suggests business
sense.
Print Run 2,000

Art Director/Studio Stan Spooner/
McMonigle & Spooner
Designer/Studio Stan Spooner/
McMonigle & Spooner
Client/Service Richard Johnson,
WesCorp, San Dimas, CA/credit
union
Paper Conqueror 24# Writing,
Wove Natural White; 40# and 28#
Gilclear
Type Cochin
Colors Three, match
Printing Offset
Software Adobe Illustrator

Concept Though part of a corporate
identity system, this letterhead for the
CEO of the nation's largest credit
union is also intensely personal. The
colors and wave pattern are straight
from the identity standards, but the
Chinese characters (which read "the
wave," the prime graphic image in
the company's new identity) reflect
Mr. Johnson's long career in the U.S.
Marines and his interest in Chinese
culture. They also display his talent in
Chinese calligraphy—he wrote them
himself.
Special Visual Effect The unusual
size of the paper draws attention to its
transparency. The designer chose the
translucent stock for its resemblance
to rice paper.
Print Run 2,000

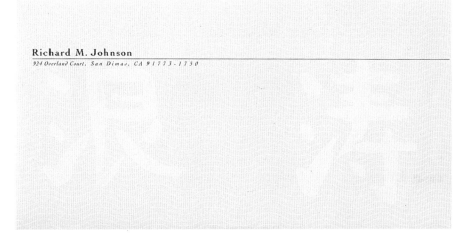

Art Director/Studio Jack Anderson/
Hornall Anderson Design Works
Designers/Studio Jack Anderson,
Scott Eggers, Leo Raymundo/Hornall
Anderson Design Works
Client/Service Mahlum & Nordfors
McKinley Gordon, Seattle, WA/
architects
Paper French Speckletone Kraft
Type Gill Sans
Colors One, black
Printing Offset
Software Aldus FreeHand, Adobe
Photoshop

Concept This temporary system was
designed to inform clients of a merg-
er. The die-cut perforations in the
corner separate the names of the two
firms from their new combined name,
humorously telling clients to tear off
the corner after the date of the merg-
er. The unbleached paper, utilitarian
type, and deceptively simple design
reinforce the letterhead's temporary
status.
Print Run 1,000

Art Director/Studio Maria Dominguez/Blue Sky Design
Designer Nicole Bailey
Illustrator Nicole Bailey
Client/Service Nicole Bailey/interior design consultant
Paper Strathmore Pastelle
Type Bodoni
Colors Two, match
Printing Offset, engraving
Software Aldus PageMaker, Aldus FreeHand

Concept To reflect the client's style of interior design, the designer used engraved images ornamented with metallic inks, thick paper with a rustic deckle edge, and die-cut business cards. Specially converted envelopes feature square flaps, adding another subtle but distinctive touch. Together the pieces imply an upscale business with exacting standards.
Cost $3,000 **Print Run** 1,000 (250 each design)

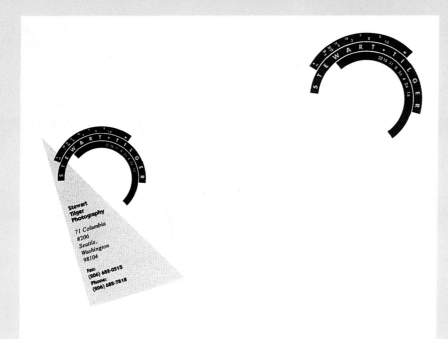

Stewart
Tilger
Photography

*71 Columbia
#206
Seattle,
Washington
98104*

Fax:
(206) 682-0515
Phone:
(206) 682-7818

Stewart
Tilger
Photography

*71 Columbia
#206
Seattle,
Washington
98104*

Art Director/Studio John Hornall/
Hornall Anderson Design Works
Designers/Studio John Hornall,
David Bates/Hornall Anderson
Design Works
Client/Service Stewart Tilger
Photography, Seattle, WA/
photographer
Paper Strathmore Writing
Type Futura (logo), Kabel (name),
Caslon 540 Italic (address)
Colors Three, match
Printing Offset
Software Aldus FreeHand

Concept Artistic renderings of camera components mark this letterhead
package for a photographer. Camera
dials, skewed to represent their being
set for a photograph, make an intriguing graphic that suggests the photographer's skill and professionalism. A
gray screen dividing the letterhead
into two triangles represents light and
shadow. The business cards repeat
the image in an innovative way: A
black triangle printed on the back of
the translucent vellum paper creates a
gray triangle on the right side,
beneath the type.
Print Run 1,500

ANDY ZANGORILLA

ANDY ZANGRILLI

President

DANTE'S RESTAURANTS, INC.

936 E. College Ave.

State.College, PA 16801

814-234-1344

Fax 814-237-2925

Gullifty's

Mario & Luigis

The Deli

Hi-Way Pizza Pubs

The Saloon

Taton

ANDY ZANGORILLA

ANDY ZANGRILLI
DANTE'S RESTAURANTS, INC.
936 E. College Ave.
State College, PA 16801

ANDY ZANGORILLA

ANDY ZANGRILLI

President
DANTE'S RESTAURANTS, INC.
936 E. College Ave.
State College, PA 16801
814-234-1344
Fax 814-237-2925

Art Directors/Studio Lanny
Sommese, Kristin Sommese/
Sommese Design
Designer/Studio Kristin Sommese/
Sommese Design
Illustrator Lanny Sommese
Client/Service Andy Zangrilli, State
College, PA/restaurateur
Paper Cross Pointe Genesis
Type Emigre Matrix Narrow,
Senator Ultra and Demi
Printing Offset
Software Aldus PageMaker

Concept A nickname inspired this
humorous package that features a
foldout business card. The client's
friends called him "Zangorilla," natural fodder for cartoons. The folded
card pictures a mild-mannered gorilla
beneath the client's nickname.
Unfolded, the card reveals the gorilla
bearing a covered dish, wine glass
and towel. This image is repeated on
letterhead and envelopes. Because the
foldout card cost more than a traditional flat card, the designers econo-
mized by using only one ink color.
Different paper colors add variety
without adding expense.

Art Director/Studio Calvin Lew/
Calvin Lew Design
Designer/Studio Calvin Lew/Calvin
Lew Design
Illustration Calvin Lew
Client/Service Louie's Construction,
San Francisco, CA/general contractor
Paper Simpson Quest White
Type Adobe Garamond Expert
Colors Two, match
Printing Offset, foil stamping
Software Adobe Photoshop, Aldus
FreeHand, QuarkXPress

Concept The logo is of paramount
importance in this package, because
the client's clients are both Asian and
American. The classic type is pleasantly neutral, allowing the logo to
command attention. Foil stamping
adds extra emphasis. The system
refers to all basic building materials:
the foil representing steel, the printed
square representing wood, and the
textured paper representing concrete.
Cost-Saving Technique The designer
kept the logo the same size on all
pieces, so the printer needed only one
foil-stamping die.
Cost $3,500 **Print Run** 1,000

Art Director/Studio Steve Spazuk/
Tarzan Communication Graphique
Designers/Studio George Fok,
Daniel Fortin/Tarzan Communication
Graphique
Photographer Adrien Duey
Client/Service Tarzan
Communication Graphique,
Montreal, Quebec, Canada/graphic
design
Paper Parilux, Cream
Type Garamond, hand-lettering
Colors Four, process
Printing Offset
Software Adobe Photoshop, Adobe
Illustrator

Concept The designers wanted to
convey the spirit of their design phi-
losophy: reinvesting art in design.
Their letterhead system, which continues the colors used in their offices,
includes intriguing art and die cuts. In
the logo, the word "art" appears in
the shadow of the firm's name. The
paper appeals to the hand with its
heavy clay coating as well as its wav-
ing edges. Even the envelopes continue the distinctive curves on their
sides and flaps.
Print Run 2,000

IMPRESSIONS

A Quality

Improvement

Process

of Williamson

Printing

Corporation

6700

Denton Drive

Dallas

Texas 75235

Telephone

214

902 2700

IONS

A Quality Improvement Process of Williamson Printing Corporation

Williamson

Printing

Corporation

6700

Denton Drive

Dallas

Texas 75235

Art Directors/Studio Todd Hart, Shawn Freeman/Focus 2
Designer/Studio Shawn Freeman/Focus 2
Client/Service Williamson Printing Co., Dallas, TX/four-color printer
Paper Simpson Starwhite Vicksburg
Type Adobe Garamond
Colors Two, match
Printing Offset, foil stamping
Software QuarkXPress

Concept Although many printers opt for saturated colors and complicated layouts to demonstrate their abilities, this printer wanted something more restrained. Fine paper and the precise, thin lines of the small type show the printer's commitment to quality workmanship; foil stamping the first part of the word "Impressions" adds an upscale touch—like debossing, but with a contemporary twist—that's also appropriate to the word it depicts.
Cost $6,000 **Print Run** 10,000

Directory of Design Firms

246 Fifth Design Inc.
246 Fifth Avenue
Ottawa, Ontario K15 2N3
CANADA

Adletera Design Studio
13430 NW Hwy, Ste. 609
Houston, TX 77040

After Hours
1201 E. Jefferson, #B100
Phoenix, AZ 85034

Agency X
9867 Shoreham
Los Angeles, CA 90069

Ant Design
622 Village Green Ln. W
Madison, WI 53704

Artis Werbe-Consulting
Occamstrasse 4
80802 Munchen
GERMANY

Blue Sky Design
6401 SW 132 Ct. Circle
Miami, FL 33183

Boelts Bros. Design
14 E. 2nd Street
Tucson, AZ 85705

The Bottom Line
56 Park Lake Street
Orlando, FL 32803

Brand Design Co.
814 N. Harrison Street
Wilmington, DE 19806

Brazell Design
11447 S. 46th Street
Phoenix, AZ 85044

Carolyn Brown Design
513 W. Clapier Street
Philadelphia, PA 19144

RM Brünz Studio
PO Box 454
Issaquah, WA 98027

Julie Bush Design
1164 N. Dearborn, #416
Chicago, IL 60610

Circle Design Inc.
200-72 Princess Street
Winnipeg, Manitoba R3B 1K2
CANADA

Trudy Cole-Zielanski Design
Rt. 1 Box 362
Mount Solon, VA 22843

V. Allen Crawford Design
174 Jordan Road
Somers Point, NJ 08244

The Dunlavey Studio Inc.
3576 McKinley Blvd.
Sacramento, CA 95816

Maureen Erbe Design
1948 S. La Cienega Blvd.
Los Angeles, CA 90034

Eye Noise
1215 East Robinson Street
Orlando, FL 32801

Barbara Ferguson Designs
10211 Swanton Drive
Santee, CA 92071

Fish & Co.
2461 A Street
San Diego, CA 92102

Focus2
2105 Commerce #100
Dallas, TX 75201

Free Range Chicken Ranch
330A E. Campbell Ave.
Campbell, CA 95008

Fresh Squeezed Design
3100 13th Ave. So., #302
Fargo, ND 58103

Kathryn Frund Design
4 Glover Avenue
Newtown, CT 06470

Earl Gee Design
501 Second Street, Ste. 700
San Francisco, CA 94107

Grafik Communications
1199 N. Fairfax, Ste. 700
Alexandria, VA 22314

Half Moon Design Co.
PO Box 4428
Jackson Hole, WY 83001

Mara Hines Design
625 Summer Street, PO Box 432
Marshfield Hills, MA 02051

Hornall Anderson Design Works
1008 Western Street, Ste. 600
Seattle, WA 98104

Image Factory
19 W. Flagler, Ste. 301
Miami, FL 33130

Images
1835 Hampden Court
Louisville, KY 40205

Jager DiPaola Kemp Design
308 Pine Street
Burlington, VT 05401

Joven Orozco Design
10222 Saddle Hill Terrace
Alta Loma, CA 91737

Eric Kass Design
9645 Alexander Lane
Fishers, IN 46038

Killer Creative
4170 Ashford-Dunwoody Rd.,
Ste. 570
Atlanta, GA 30319

Klassen Graphic Designs
316 Congress
Austin, TX 78701

KODE Associates Inc.
54 West 22nd Street, 4th floor
New York, NY 10010

Carolyn Lastick Design
426 N. Essex Ave.
Nalberth, PA 19072

Calvin Lew Design
3112 Pinole Valley Rd.
Pinole, CA 94564

Lundy.Keetle
2 Church Street, Ste. 2A
Burlington, VT 05401

M Design
46 Waltham Street, Studio 603
Boston, MA 02118

Magic {8} Design
3445 Bradley Place
Raleigh, NC 27607

McMonigle & Spooner
818 E. Foothill
Monrovia, CA 91016

Miller Brooks
11712 N. Michigan Rd.
Zionsville, IN 46077

Mires Design Inc.
2345 Kettner Blvd.
San Diego, CA 92101

Modern Dog
601 Valley Street, #309
Seattle, WA 98109

Niche Design Group
175 Brunswick Street
Fitzroy, Vic 3065
AUSTRALIA

O&J Design, Inc.
9 West 29th Street
New York, NY 10001

O'Hare Design
1940 10th Ave., Suite B
Vero Beach, FL 32960

Peat Jariya Design
1601 Woodhead
Houston, TX 77019

Pentagram Design
212 Fifth Avenue
New York, NY 10010

Peterson & Co.
2200 N. Lamar, S-310
Dallas, TX 75202

Phippen Design Group
2200 Bridgeway
Sausalito, CA 94965

Phoenix Creative
611 North Tenth
Saint Louis, MO 63101

Pierce Design
953 Acapulco Street
Laguna Beach, CA 92651

Potomac Communications
3925 Jenifer Street NW
Washington, DC 20015

Quoi de Neuf? Communication
3315 France Prime Suite 713
Ste-Foy, Quebec G1W 4X3
CANADA

Richards & Swensen
350 S. 400 E., Ste. 300
Salt Lake City, UT 84111

Riddell Advertising and Design
Gas Light Alley, PO Box 2962
Jackson Hole, WY 83001

Sackett Design
864 Folsom Street
San Francisco, CA 94107

Sayles Graphic Design
308 Eighth Street
Des Moines, IA 50309

Schowalter 2 Design
21 The Crescent
Short Hills, NJ 07078

Rick Sealock Design
112 C 17th Ave. NW
Calgary, Alberta T2M OM6
CANADA

Siebert Design
1600 Sycamore Street
Cincinnati, OH 45202

Susan Smith Illustration
537 Chestnut Street
Needham, MA 02192

Sommese Design
481 Glenn Road
State College, PA 16803

Steelhaus
4991 Eller Road
Chattanooga, TN 37416

Clifford Stoltze Design
49 Melcher Street, 4th Flr.
Boston, MA 02210

Studio MD
1512 Alaskan Way
Seattle, WA 98101

Suburbia Studios
53 Tovey Cr.
Victoria, BC V9B 1A4
CANADA

SullivanPerkins
2811 McKinney Ave., Ste. 320,
LB111
Dallas, TX 75204

Supon Design Group
1000 Connecticut Ave. NW, #415
Washington, DC 20036

Tarzan Communication Graphique
20 Marie-Anne Ouest
Montreal, Quebec H2W 1B5
CANADA

Thibault Paolini Design Assoc.
19 Commercial Street
Portland, ME 04101

Janice Troutman-Rains Design
1523 8th Street
Cuyahoga Falls, OH 44221

Wet Paper Bag
6421 Arthur Drive
Ft. Worth, TX 76134

White Design
4500 E. Pacific Coast Highway #320
Long Beach, CA 90747

Wordsmiths
5950 Canoga Ave., #420
Woodland Hills, CA 91367

Cindy Wrobel Design & Illustration
415 Alta Dena
Street Louis, MO 63130

Zappata Diseñadores
Lafayete 143 Anzures
Mexico City
MEXICO 11590

Index of Design Firms

Index of Clients

Copyright Notices

All images have been reproduced with the knowledge and consent of the artists concerned.

Page 12 (left) © Julie Bush Design.

Page 12 (right) © Joven Orozco.

Page 13 © Eye Noise, Inc.

Page 14 © 1994 Lewis Glaser/Wet Paper Bag Graphic Design.

Page 15 © Magic {8} Design.

Page 16 © Potomac Communications.

Page 17 © 1992 Steven Trank Photography.

Page 18 © Mara Hines Graphic Design.

Page 19 © David Hernandez.

Page 20 © Jager Di Paola Kemp Design.

Page 21 © Adcetera Design Studio.

Page 22 © Nicholas Pedneault.

Page 23 © Schowalter 2 Design.

Page 24 © Carolyn Brown.

Page 25 © Trudy Cole-Zielanski.

Page 26 © Earl Gee Design.

Page 27 © Maureen Erbe Design.

Page 28 © Susan Smith.

Page 29 © Miller Brooks, Inc.

Page 30 © RM Brünz Studio.

Page 31 © Cindy Wrobel.

Page 32 © Armstrong Creative.

Page 33 © Riddell Advertising & Design.

Page 34 © 1994 Peterson & Company.

Page 35 © Troutman Rains Design.

Page 36 © Allen Crawford Design.

Page 37 © 1993 Mike Grandmaison.

Page 38 © Phoenix Creative.

Page 39 © Rick Sealock.

Page 40 © 1993 After Hours Creative.

Page 41 © RM Brünz Studio.

Page 42 © Focus 2.

Page 43 © Eric Kass Design.

Page 44 © 1992 Barbara Ferguson.

Page 45 © Focus 2.

Page 46 © Stoltze Design.

Page 47 © 1993 Magdalena Dukeland.

Page 48 © Peterson & Company.

Page 49 © 1993 Lundy Keetle.

Page 50 © Peterson & Company.

Page 51 © Riddell Advertising & Design.

Page 54 (top) © Earl Gee Design.

Page 54 (middle) © Carolyn Lastick Design.

Page 54 (bottom) © 246 Fifth Design Inc.

Page 55 © 1993 Russell Pierce.

Page 56 © Steelhaus.

Page 57 © Sayles Graphic Design.

Page 58 © Supon Design Group, Inc.

Page 59 © Boelts Bros. Design Inc.

Page 60 © Suburbia Studio Ltd.

Page 61 © Pentagram Design and Gwen Baker.

Page 62 © 1993 Artis Consulting.

Page 63 © 1994 Modern Dog.

Page 64 © Richards & Swensen.

Page 65 © White Design.

Page 66 © Sayles Graphic Design.

Page 67 © One Fifth Avenue.

Page 68 © 1993 Brand Design Company Inc.

Page 69 © Blue Sky Design.

Page 70 © Atomic Ironworks.

Page 71 © Sackett Design Associates.

Page 72 © 1993 Earth Products, Inc.

Page 73 © Killer Creative Design Studio.

Page 74 © Hornall Anderson Design Works.

Page 75 © 1992 Grafik Communications.

Page 76 © Boelts Bros. Design.

Page 77 © Tarzan Communication Graphique

Page 80 (top) © Agency X.

Page 80 (middle) © Mires Design, Inc.

Page 80 (bottom) © 1994 River City Brewing Company.

Page 81 © 1993 Modern Dog.

Page 82 © Siebert Design Inc.

Page 83 © Suburbia Studios Ltd.

Page 84 © 1993 Stoltze Design.

Page 85 © Wordsmiths Advertising.

Page 86 © Fresh Squeezed Design.

Page 87 © Riddell Advertising & Design.

Page 88 © Sackett Design Associates and Donnelly & Associates.

Page 89 © 1992 [Metal] Studio, Inc.

Page 90 © Niche Design Group.

Page 91 © 246 Fifth Design, Inc.

Page 92 © Focus 2.

Page 93 © 246 Fifth Design, Inc.

Page 94 © M Design.

Page 95 © The Walt Disney Company.

Page 96 © Sayles Graphic Design.

Page 97 © Zappata Diseñadores.

Page 98 © Schowalter 2 Design.

Page 99 © 1993 52nd District Agriculture Association, Sacramento, CA.

Page 100 © Free Range Chicken Ranch.

Page 101 © 1993 The National Museum of the American Indian.

Page 102 © Carol F. Chamberlin.

Page 103 © Mires Design, Inc.

Page 104 © Sackett Design Associates.

Page 105 © 1993 Julius Friedman, Images.

Page 106 © Austin Natural Science Association and Dinamation International Inc.

Page 107 © 1994 World of Good Tastes, Sacramento, CA.

Page 108 © 1993 California Association of Winegrape Growers, Sacramento, CA.

Page 109 © 1993 Thibault Paolini Design Associates and Barbara Emmons.

Page 110 © The Bottom Line Advertising & Design.

Page 111 © Sackett Design Associates and Kim Howard Illustration.

Page 114 (left) © Tarzan Communication Graphique.

Page 114 (center) © KODE Associates.

Page 114 (right) © The Jollymen.

Page 115 (left) © O'Hare Design, Inc.

Page 115 (center) card and logo © B & G Painting; photograph © Phippen Design Group.

Page 115 (right) © Fish & Co.

Page 116 © Print Northwest/Six Sigma and Hornall Anderson Design Works.

Page 117 © Tarzan Communication Graphique

Page 118 © 1993 Lundy.Keetle.

Page 119 © Tarzan Communication Graphique

Page 120 © O'Hare Design, Inc.

Page 121 © Image Factory - Advertising.

Page 122 © Studio MD.

Page 123 © O&J Design, Inc.

Page 124 © Richard Johnson and McMonigle & Spooner.

Page 125 © Mahlum & Nordfors McKinley Gordon and Hornall Anderson Design Works.

Page 126 © Blue Sky Design.

Page 127 © Stewart Tilger Photography and Hornall Anderson Design Works.

Page 128 © Sommese Design.

Page 129 © Calvin Lew Design.

Page 130 © Tarzan Communication Graphique

Page 131 © Focus 2.

More Great Books for Knock-Out Graphic Design!